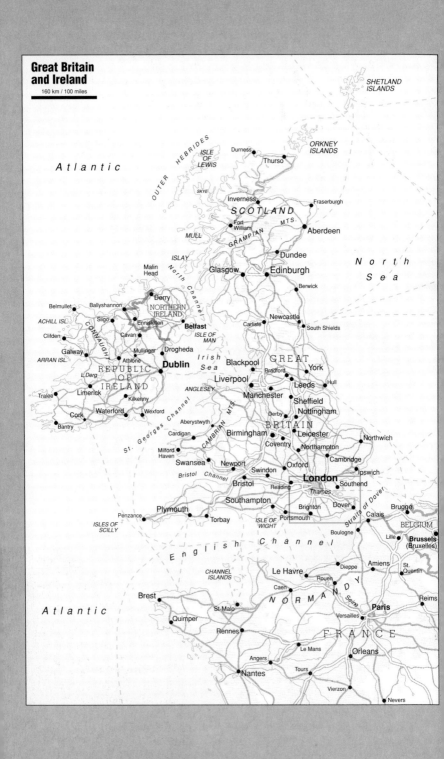

Great Britain and Ireland

160 km / 100 miles

Welcome!

This is a guide to the very best of Southeast England, an area noted for its splendid stately homes and outstanding gardens, its tranquil and varied landscapes, its attractive villages and towns. Your guide to the region is Christopher Catling, author of books on travel, gardening and antiques, who lives in rural East Sussex and knows the area intimately. Drawing on his detailed local knowledge, Christopher will show you the highlights of the region and recommend the best places for food, accommodation and shopping. His carefully planned itineraries provide the basis for a rewarding week or fortnight's touring.

The itineraries take the form of a circular tour starting in the ancient cathedral city of Canterbury. From there you follow the North Downs and visit a succession of magnificent houses and palaces: Leeds Castle rising romantically from its island in a lake; Knole with its Jacobean interiors and deer park; the world-famous gardens at Sissinghurst; Winston Churchill's former home at Chartwell and Anne Boleyn's treasure-filled castle at Hever.

The castle town of Lewes marks the westernmost point in your journey and serves as the base for excursions to Brighton, Chichester, Glyndebourne and the former homes of Virginia Woolf, Vanessa Bell and Duncan Grant.

The return journey takes in the soaring cliffs and nature reserves of Cuckmere Haven and Seven Sisters, the site of the Battle of Hastings and the house where Rudyard Kipling wrote *Puck of Pook's Hill*. From the cobbled streets of the ancient Cinque Port town of Rye, the final stage of your tour takes you across the bird-filled wilderness of Romney Marsh to the Channel Tunnel terminal and ends on the famous White Cliffs of Dover.

These itineraries reveal the richness of an area that is easily reached from London or the Channel Ports and yet remains remarkably unspoiled, a rural idyll that will appeal to anyone who takes pleasure in traditional English landscapes and architecture.

Welcome!

Insight Pocket Guide:

SOUTHEAST ENGLAND

First Edition

INSIGHT *Pocket* GUIDES

SOUTH EAST ENGLAND

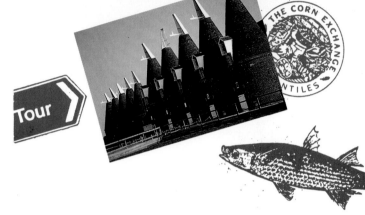

Tour ❯

THE CORN EXCHANGE
NTILES

Author **Christopher Catling**
Photographer **Robert Mort**

INSIGHT
Pocket
GUIDES

Contents

Chichester
Cathedral

Maps

Dear Reader

On my first visit to Southeast England I realised that I had been here before – not in some previous incarnation, but in my imagination, fed from an early age by the idyllic summer landscapes celebrated in *Winnie the Pooh*, *Puck of Pook's Hill*, and the poetry of Hilaire Belloc. A A Milne, Rudyard Kipling and Belloc were just three of the many authors who were inspired by the region's timeless and tranquil landscapes. Another was the visionary, William Blake, who penned the words to his immortal *Jerusalem*, England's unofficial national anthem, as he gazed up at the South Downs from his cottage window in Felpham:

> And did those feet in ancient time
> Walk upon England's mountains green?
> And was the holy Lamb of God
> On England's pleasant pastures seen?

Blake would be apoplectic if he could see the appalling urban sprawl that hems his cottage in today and which has ruined so much of the south coast. Yet the more rural parts of Kent and East and West Sussex that I intend to show you in this guide would still be recognisable to Blake and Kipling, not to mention the host of other thinkers, writers and artists who have found refuge here and the stimulus to produce their best works; Henry James, Virginia Woolf, Maynard Keynes, Duncan Grant, Vanessa Bell, H E Bates and E F Benson, to name but a few (and to bring the list up to date, my near neighbours today include Paul and Linda McCartney, Spike Milligan, Derek Jarman and Roger Daltrey).

The fact that so much of Southeast England remains rural and unspoiled, despite the proximity of London, is partly to do with the topography and partly to do with the conservatism of local

people. The soils are, for the most part, heavy clay and difficult to plough. Prairie farms are rare and the landscape is a patchwork of woodland, orchards and pasture in which wildflowers flourish and ancient timber-framed farms, with redbrick barns and white-capped oast houses, look as natural as if they, too, had grown out of the soil. This is smallholding country where countless farmers earn a meagre living from rearing sheep and cows, from coppicing, horticulture, hops and fruit – the reason why the region is sometimes called 'the Garden of England'. These activities will never make them rich, but they love their work and would be reluctant to change it for a City income and a BMW in the garage.

Conservative they may be, but local people are not narrow-minded; many an incomer has found a warm welcome here – myself included – and several of the nursery gardens, fruit farms, vineyards and village shops near to me are run by Dutch, German and Scandinavian families, people who came here as visitors, liked what they found and decided to stay.

How many more will follow their example? You perhaps? Will Southeast England become a bridgehead to the new Europe? The planners certainly hope so, and have schemes on the drawing board to transform the region into the hub of a Europe-wide distribution network, linked to the Continent via the Channel Tunnel. Will the essential character of Southeast England survive such momentous change? Only time will tell, but I strongly recommend that you set out to explore the region while it retains its allure, just in case...

The Legacy of Conquest

At the Straits of Dover, England and France are only 20 miles/32km apart. Even such a short stretch of water has proved an invaluable barrier against invasion, and kept at bay the armies of Napoleon and Hitler which had swept inexorably across mainland Europe. But the Romans and the Normans made the crossing successfully and southeast England became the theatre for decisive battles.

Roman villa mosaic

Caesar first came over to England in 55BC, landing at Deal, not far from where visitors disembark from cross-Channel ferries today. Caesar was not made welcome and timed his foray badly; equinoctial gales damaged his ships and he only stayed long enough to undertake repairs before retreating to Gaul. He returned the following year and stayed for two months, marching northward to the Thames and winning a few easy battles against local tribal leaders who agreed to pay tribute to Rome.

Like all politicians, Caesar was prone to exaggeration and claimed to have conquered Britain. In reality Britain remained independent and prosperous, exporting wheat, horses, tin and gold to the Roman Empire. But why should Rome pay for British raw materials when the Roman military machine was more than adequate to conquer these northern isles? Some pretext had to be found for an invasion, of course: were not the Belgic chiefs of southern England fomenting dissent against Roman rule in northern Gaul – today's Brittany?

Culture

Grave of a Roman officer

This was good enough reason for the emperor Claudius to dispatch his general Aulus Plautius on a mission of conquest. He landed at Richborough on the Kent coast in AD43 and began a forty-year military campaign. Dover became a major port where supply ships docked bringing reinforcements; the Roman *pharos*, or lighthouse, still stands alongside the castle and the road from Dover to Canterbury follows the route the Romans built for troop movements.

Roman rule lasted four centuries, but its grip was increasingly tenuous from the third century, when Canterbury's massive flint walls were built. Saxon pirates from the upper Rhineland raided the southeast coast with increasing ferocity until, in AD410, after the Roman army had been pulled out to defend territory closer to home, the Saxons staged their own conquest.

Bayham Abbey, victim of Henry VIII's dissolution

Of Saxon culture little remains, in contrast to the Roman pottery, mosaics and bronzework that fill the archaeological museums at Canterbury and Lewes. The Saxons were master craftsmen in wood, building graceful longboats and massive longhouses, most of which have long biodegraded, leaving little clue to their culture. They are portrayed by late Roman writers as violent and tyrannical barbarians – but that is how you would expect Rome's enemies to be portrayed. Life in Saxon southeast England could not have been too inhospitable, since Saint Augustine founded a substantial monastery at Canterbury in AD598, the remains of which survive, and began his task of converting the

Caesar's landing

Saxon people to Christianity.

One great masterpiece of late Saxon art has survived but you will have to go all the way to Normandy to see it. *The Bayeux Tapestry* was commissioned by Bishop Odo of Bayeux, who became Earl of Kent after the Norman Conquest, and embroidered by English needleworkers – possibly the nuns of Minster-in-Sheppey, north of Canterbury. It is a simple work of propaganda, created in order to justify the Conquest. William, Duke of Normandy, claimed that Edward the Confessor had nominated him to the English throne. The tapestry shows Harold Godwinson, Earl of Wessex, the main rival claimant, being dispatched as an emissary to Normandy, and swearing on the Bible to support William's claim to the throne.

When Edward died, Godwinson was crowned king, thereby breaking his holy oath, and William received papal sanction for his invasion of England. The decisive battle between Normans and Saxons was fought in October 1066 on the spot known ever since as Battle (*Day 6*) and William founded an abbey here to atone for the bloodshed – the first of hundreds of superb buildings constructed by the Normans in England.

Martyrs and Pilgrims

In William's time, Church and state effectively operated as one and reinforced each other but, as the Norman rulers began to establish a framework of civil law – a framework which still forms the basis

William the Conqueror's arrival (Bayeux Tapestry)

of the English legal system – the existence of separate ecclesiastical courts proved a source of constant friction. The Church claimed exclusive jurisdiction over its property and members, clerics in holy orders. Ecclesiastical courts were suspected of treating clerical misdemeanours too leniently, and it was almost impossible for civilians to sue the Church for alleged grievances.

When Henry II appointed Thomas Becket, Archbishop of Canterbury, he fully expected his best friend, the man who had been his chancellor and to whom he had entrusted the education of his son, to stand with him in challenging the authority of the Church. Instead, Becket became committed to the papal position and the king's impetuous demand to know 'Who will rid me of this turbulent priest?' was read as an instruction to assassinate Becket.

The four knights who killed him in Canterbury cathedral on 29 December 1170 achieved the opposite of their intentions. The murder of an anointed archbishop on consecrated ground caused outrage which the Church exploited to its advantage. Henry was forced to do public penance at Becket's tomb and his shrine became one of the most famous in Christendom until Henry VIII, who ended papal authority in England, ordered its destruction in 1538.

Canterbury pilgrims

Building Boom

About the time Chaucer began his *Canterbury Tales* (1387), southeast England was undergoing a transformation. French raids on coastal towns continued but more in the spirit of piracy and plunder than serious invasion. Relative peace led to new styles in domestic architecture.

Some buildings were still defensive: Bodiam Castle (*Day 6*), begun in 1385, is one example but archaeologists who have recently surveyed the surrounding earthworks now think they represent garden remains, rather than military entrenchment, an indication that Bodiam was built as much for aesthetics as defence.

Meanwhile, at Penshurst (*Day 3*) Sir John de Pulteney built a princely manor house without fortification of any kind, although fortified walls were added after 1393. The great hall at Penshurst, designed for communal living, has been preserved exactly as it was built, around 1341, the best surviving example of medieval domestic building in England. Pulteney was a rich man, a merchant who was four times Lord Mayor of London. A humbler, though still impressive, house of the same period survives at Alfriston: the Clergy House, built for the parish priest, is a Wealden-type, so called be-

Alfriston vicarage which dates from Chaucer's time

cause its characteristic feature, jetted side wings, is most commonly found in the Wealden area of southeast England.

A large number of Wealden medieval hall houses have survived and you will often be stopped in your tracks by the sight of some perfect gem of timber framing. They owe their survival to the durable and plentiful chestnut and oak of which they were built and to economic decline during the Industrial Revolution when coal and steel replaced the Weald's natural resources of charcoal, timber and iron, and production shifted farther north.

This decline meant that few people had the wealth to tear down their medieval houses and replace them in newly fashionable brick, though in towns like Lewes (*Day 4*), brick or tile facades were added to timber structures to make them more fashionably Georgian. If you stop to admire the charm of the region's medieval farmhouses, you find that most of them are roofed with handmade clay tiles, the colour of a robin's breast. The roofs are very steep and many are carried down to within a few feet of the ground – locally known as cat-slide roofs. In the words of the late architectural historian, Alec Clifton-Taylor, 'These gently billowing eiderdowns of mellow terracotta red offer an experience of colour and texture of quite exceptional richness.'

Architects and Gardeners

Not every timber building covered in gorgeous terracotta is medieval, though. Southeast England was the early stamping ground of the great architect Edwin Lutyens, who designed many new buildings in the local vernacular style and, as at Great Dixter (*Day 6*) rescued genuine medieval structures, incorporating them into his own projects. Lutyens set a style that was widely copied by architects who preferred the homeliness of the vernacular to the urbanity of Modernism.

The period up to the mid-1930s was the last time that true craftsmanship in wood flourished in this country and you will see many examples of what used to be dismissed contemptuously as 'mock Tudor', from the beautifully made oak doors of Sissinghurst Castle, to the outstanding carving at Hever Castle.

Gertrude Jekyll created the garden style

Servant's quarters in Hever Castle

Servant's quarters in Hever Castle

that is instantly recognisable today as English. Her influence is especially evident at Goodnestone Park (*Day 1*) and Sissinghurst (*Day 3*), and even modern gardens such as Denmans (*Day 4*) and Great Dixter (*Day 6*) follow her ideas in their use of mixed borders, naturalistic planting and wild areas within a formal framework.

Artists and Writers

Throw a stone in Sussex, local people say, and there is a very strong chance you will hit an author or artist. If you want to see just how many well-known writers, living and dead, sought inspiration from the region's unspoilt countryside, visit the Martello Bookshop in Rye (*Day 7*) and look at the list on the bookshop notice board. The reason is that nowhere else in England can you enjoy rural tranquillity and find attractive, affordable houses so close to the cultural stimulus of London.

Not that every author who settled here had to worry about house prices. Rudyard Kipling could afford one of the finest residences in the region (Bateman's, *Day 6*), and a chauffeur-driven

The magnificent medieval palace of Penshurst

Rolls-Royce. Both Henry James and E F Benson lived in Rye's finest town house. But Virginia Woolf wrote with freezing fingers in a relatively nondescript house in Rodmell (*Day 4*), unable for several years to afford adequate heating. Her sister, Vanessa Bell, and her Bloomsbury coterie rented a farmhouse at Charleston (*Day 4*), painting busily to distract herself from money worries. D H Lawrence wrote *The Rainbow* in a humble converted cow byre at Greatham (adjacent to Parham House, *Day 4*).

The ghosts of other writers haunt every corner of southeast England. Gibbon, author of *The Decline and Fall of the Roman Empire*, ended his days at Sheffield Park (*Day 4*), Malcolm Lowry at Ripe, near Lewes, and Arthur Conan Doyle at Crowborough, near Tunbridge Wells. Gilbert White's *Natural History* is as much a study of the South Downs around Ringmer, near Lewes, where he often stayed, as it is of his home village at Selborne; and Hilaire Belloc wrote much of his verse at Shipley, West Sussex.

Virginia Woolf

Another local author, H E Bates, lived and wrote at Little Chart, just south of Charing (*Day 2*), between 1931 and his death in 1974. He saw this idyllic stretch of countryside, where pilgrims once walked on their way to Canterbury, cut off from the Downs by the M20 motorway. Running along the same motorway is a railway line that will soon form the main high-speed rail link between London and the Channel Tunnel and thence to all parts of Continental Europe. The adjacent town of Ashford will be the English hub of the European rail network.

Bates foresaw this and was angry. His Larkin family novels are a celebration of all that he valued in the countryside and all that he feared would be destroyed. With its woodlands, heath, downland and coast, its mild climate and traditional farming methods, the region retains abundant wildlife, although this is increasingly becoming isolated in special reserves maintained by conservation bodies. The words of Pop Larkin, Bates's central character, still ring true: when asked why he objects to the construction of a new road, Larkin replies: 'Ah, you should be here in spring… Blackbirds, nightingales, primroses, millions of bluebells – Perfick little bit of England. Perfick'.

Historical Highlights

55BC Caesar conquers southeast England and forces local chieftains to pay tribute to Rome.

AD43 Aulus Plautius arrives to conquer the rest of Britain. Southeast England becomes the 'granary of the empire'.

3rd century Saxons raid the southeast coast; Romans build defensive walls around cities and establish a string of shore forts.

410 Saxons conquer southeast England and settle in the Romney Marsh area.

597 Saint Augustine is sent to convert England to Christianity and sets up base in Canterbury.

1066 William, Duke of Normandy, defeats Saxon king Harold at the Battle of Hastings and is crowned king of England.

1070 Lanfranc, the first Norman archbishop of Canterbury, begins a huge new cathedral.

1170 Becket murdered in Canterbury cathedral which is rebuilt as his shrine.

1264 The Battle of Lewes. Simon de Montfort defeats Henry III and summons a parliament of barons, knights, clergy and two representatives of every English borough, sowing the seeds of parliamentary democracy.

1283 Edward I creates the town of Winchelsea as a port for the wine trade with Gascony.

1336 Henry III officially designates Rye as a Cinque Port, the first line of defence against raids from France.

1535 Henry VIII declares himself head of the English Church and seizes monastic property; abbeys such as Canterbury, Battle, Bayham and Lewes are dismantled for building materials.

17th century The region reaches the peak of prosperity as the centre of iron-smelting and charcoal-producing industries.

18th century Closure of many iron furnaces leads to unemployment and unrest and formation of smuggling gangs to evade duties on brandy, lace and tobacco.

1774 Tom Paine, an excise officer in Lewes, is sacked for publishing a pamphlet calling for more resources to combat smuggling. He departs for America.

1783 Prince Regent visits Brighton and builds a villa, beginning the fashion for seaside holidays.

1805 The southeast coast is fortified against Napoleonic invasion which never occurs. Martello Towers, modelled on the Torre della Martella in Corsica, built by Royal Engineers. Royal Military Canal dug from Rye to Hythe to assist with troop movements.

1919 Virginia Woolf moves to Rodmell where she lives until her suicide in the River Ouse in 1941.

1930 Vita Sackville-West and Harold Nicholson move to Sissinghurst Castle.

1939–45 Martello Towers used as World War II anti-aircraft batteries whilst the Battle of Britain is fought above. Churchill directs wartime operations from secret tunnels below Dover Castle.

1947 The first Town and Country Planning Act is introduced because of destructive development along the southeast coast.

1958 The pressure of development continues with the upgrading of Gatwick to become London's second airport.

1994 Projected opening date for the Channel Tunnel.

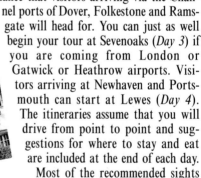

Southeast England consists of the four counties (from east to west) of Kent, East Sussex, Surrey and West Sussex. This is one of the richest areas in England for gardens and stately homes, churches, abbeys and castles. Over 120 places of interest are open to the public. The itineraries covered by Days 1 to 7 show the best of the region over a week, at a leisurely pace, allowing time to enjoy the sights. If you are more energetic, you can take in some of the options or extend your tour to two weeks.

The itineraries take the form of a circular tour, which you can join at any point. Day 1 begins at Canterbury, simply because this is the first town of importance that visitors arriving via the Channel ports of Dover, Folkestone and Ramsgate will head for. You can just as well begin your tour at Sevenoaks (*Day 3*) if you are coming from London or Gatwick or Heathrow airports. Visitors arriving at Newhaven and Portsmouth can start at Lewes (*Day 4*). The itineraries assume that you will drive from point to point and suggestions for where to stay and eat are included at the end of each day. Most of the recommended sights are open from Easter to the end of September. Gardens and wildflowers are at their best during April to July. Late July and August is the busiest holiday period when accommodation is most difficult to find without advance booking. September can be a pleasant month to visit, with fewer crowds and the region's vast areas of woodland beginning to put on their autumn colours.

Many of the sights are administered by the National Trust and you will save money on entrance fees if you become a member; you can join at any National Trust property along the route.

DAY ①

Canterbury

Begin your tour of Southeast England in Canterbury, easily reached by fast roads from London or the Channel ports of Dover, Folkestone and Ramsgate. Recover after your journey with a leisurely walk around its medieval streets. If you have the energy, spend the afternoon at Chilham Castle, Goodnestone Park or the picturesque town of Faversham. Leave your car at the multi-storey car park in Watling Street (signposted 'Short Term Car Park' off the A2 ringroad).

Canterbury, a pilgrim's destination

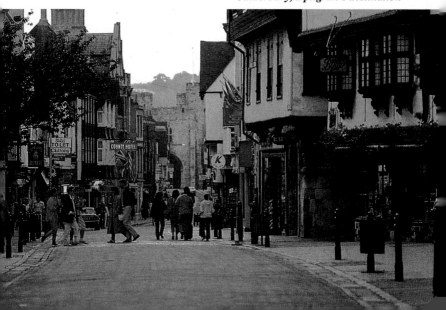

Walking around the slave market in Rome one morning, or so the story goes, Pope Gregory spotted some fair-haired children for sale and asked where they came from. Told that they were Angles (English) he replied with the memorable pun, 'Non Angli, sed angeli' (Not Angles, but angels) and promptly sent Augustine off to convert them. Augustine arrived in AD597 and set up base at Canterbury. His abbey became a major centre of learning and the cathedral which followed has been, ever since, the seat of the Archbishop of Canterbury, Primate of all England and now head of the worldwide Anglican church.

The **cathedral** was rebuilt several times, most recently after Thomas Becket was murdered in 1170, a victim of his determination not to hand over Church powers to the monarch, Henry II. St Thomas's shrine became one of the most important pilgrimage centres in Europe, and the destination of Chaucer's merry band of story-telling travellers. The city was heavily bombed during World War II (Hitler singled out Canterbury as 'the main centre of English hypocrisy' and ordered an air-strike in 1942 in retaliation for the RAF raid on Cologne). But a remarkable number of ancient buildings have survived to make Canterbury a rewarding city, full of surprises.

To reach the cathedral, leave the car park by the footbridge that leads to the Marlowe shopping centre and descend to the glass-roofed arcade below. Straight ahead is the tourist information centre, where you can pick up a free map, change money or book your overnight accommodation. Turn right down St Margaret's Street, cross the High Street and head straight for the Christ Church Gate, built in 1517 and decorated with the Tudor Rose of Henry VII. Ahead lies the soaring cathedral and it is worth spending at least an hour absorbing its details and atmosphere (open Easter to

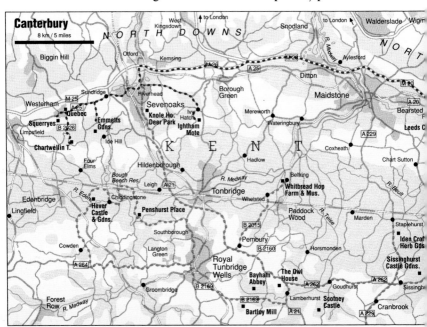

September, Monday–Friday, 8.45am–7pm; October to Easter, Monday–Friday 8.45am–5pm; Sundays all year 12.30–2.30pm and 4.30–5.30pm).

The 12th- and 13th-century stained glass, among the best of its date in Europe, rewards close study. In the **Trinity Chapel** there is an excellent sequence (dating to 1220) showing the miracles attributed to St Thomas Becket. The spot in the chapel where he was murdered is marked by a perpetually burning candle. Nearby stand the tombs of the Black Prince, portrayed in effigy in full armour, and of Henry IV.

If you want to attend Evensong check on the time at the Welcome Centre by the Christ Church Gate (usually 5.30pm weekdays, 3.30pm Saturday and Sunday); there is no better way to let the magnificence of the cathedral enter your soul than to hear the calm, ethereal music of one of England's best cathedral choirs, that of the King's School.

Enjoy the tranquillity of the cathedral precincts for a while as you explore the remains of the Great Cloister and other monastic buildings before walking east, past the King's School buildings on your left. Exit through the Quenin Gate which is cut through the Roman city walls (rebuilt in the 14th–15th centuries); go straight across Broad Street and walk down Lady Wootton's Green towards the Fyndon Gate; turn right into Monastery Street and left into Longport to reach the entrance to **St Augustine's Abbey** (open Easter to end September, 10am–6pm daily; rest of year Tuesday to Sunday 10am–4pm).

This is where Saint Augustine laid the foundations of English Christianity, establishing the monastery in AD598. It was dismantled during the Dissolution, in 1538, so all we see now is ruins, but interesting ones because they include the substantial remains of

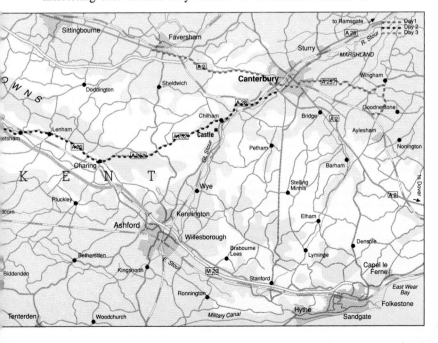

Library and museum in Canterbury

early 7th-century churches built out of reused Roman brick – in other words, you are looking at one of the very first churches to be built in England after the collapse of the Roman Empire.

Time for coffee or lunch? Turn right out of the abbey grounds up Longport, right, then first left into Church Street, cross busy Broad Street and head up Burgate Street. For coffee or a light lunch, try **Liberty's Coffee Shop**, 44 Burgate Street, or Morelli's ice cream and coffee shop opposite Christ Church Gate. Also opposite the gate is the **Olive Branch**, where you can sit at a pavement table and be entertained by buskers. Alternatively, head for the High Street where you will find a range of pubs and bistros (see *Eating Out* at the end of this section).

The High Street

When you are fortified and ready to absorb some more history, but in an entertaining way, you have a choice of two attractions. From the High Street, turn down Stour Street, beside the County Hotel, and on the right you will find **Canterbury Heritage**, a museum that takes you on a guided walk through a fine 14th-century timbered building with lively exhibits on the history of the city from Roman times to the present day (open Monday to Saturday, 10.30am–4pm (last entry) and Sundays in June to October, 1.30–4pm (last entry)). Next door, the antiques arcade is a good place to browse for old furniture, books, comics and clothes.

In St Margaret's Street you will find the **Canterbury Tales** (open April to September daily, 9.30am–5.30pm;

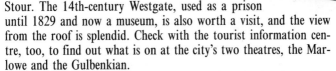

Christ Church

October to March, Monday to Friday 10am–4.30pm, Saturday and Sunday 9.30am–5.30pm) where some of the bawdier stories told by Chaucer's pilgrims are brought to life by means of tableaux, complete with farmyard smells and audio-visual tricks (commentaries in English, French, Dutch, Italian and German). Further up St Margaret's Street we return to the tourist information centre for trail leaflets which will guide you to the city's other ancient remains, such as the Castle, the Roman mosaic pavement in Butchery Lane and the Old Weaver's House with its little jetty onto the River Stour. The 14th-century Westgate, used as a prison until 1829 and now a museum, is also worth a visit, and the view from the roof is splendid. Check with the tourist information centre, too, to find out what is on at the city's two theatres, the Marlowe and the Gulbenkian.

If, on the other hand, you just want to spend the afternoon shopping, there is plenty of choice. Leading UK stores, such as Marks & Spencer, are to be found in the Marlowe Arcade. Burgate has the best of the up-market stores: Liberty, Laura Ashley, Body Shop and L'Herberie de Provence for herbal products. There are several fascinating little shops selling antiques and bric-a-brac, secondhand clothes and jewellery.

Another idea is to take a river tour, complete with student guide who will tell you about the city's history and point out some of the landmarks as he rows you down the River Stour; the embarcation point is the Old Weaver's House, by the bridge

Canterbury Cathedral

where the High Street ends and St Peter's Street begins.

Alternatively, spend the afternoon at Chilham Castle, Goodnestone Park or Faversham (see Options below), perhaps to return in time for Evensong or to explore the streets of Canterbury in the early evening when the coach parties have departed, shops and historic buildings closed and calm descends once again on the narrow streets of the city.

Tourist Information/ Accommodation Booking Service

34 St Margaret's Street
Tel: 0227-766567
Open daily 9.30am–5.30pm.

Accommodation

ABBA HOTEL

Station Road
Canterbury
Tel: 0227-464771
Pleasant, central family hotel. Moderate prices.

CATHEDRAL GATE

36 Burgate
Canterbury
Tel: 0227-464381
Opposite the main entrance to the cathedral, this hotel has real old-world charm. Moderate prices.

CHAUCER HOTEL

Ivy Lane
Canterbury
Tel: 0227-464427
Forte group hotel just outside the city walls with own car park and restaurant. Expensive.

COUNTY HOTEL

High Street
Canterbury
Tel: 0227-766266
Luxury-class hotel in the heart of the city, bedrooms in Tudor style; a good restaurant, Sulleys. Expensive.

EBURY

New Dover Road
Canterbury
Tel: 0227-768483
Family-run Victorian hotel just outside the city centre with an indoor pool. Moderate prices.

OLD COACH HOUSE

Dover Road
Barham
Tel: 0227-831218
Midway between Canterbury and Dover, with an excellent French restaurant and French-speaking staff. Moderate prices.

PILGRIMS HOTEL

18 The Friars
Canterbury
Tel: 0227-464531
Select small hotel situated opposite the Marlowe Theatre. Moderate to expensive.

POINTERS

1 London Road
Canterbury
Tel: 0227-456846
Friendly hotel in a Georgian building, 10 minutes walk from centre. Moderate prices.

WOODPECKERS

Womenswold
Tel: 0227-831319
Small country hotel midway between Dover and Canterbury set in extensive gardens. Four-poster beds, heated swimming pool and good home cooking. Moderate prices.

Eating Out

Canterbury lacks up-market gourmet restaurants but has a large number of pubs selling homemade pies, casseroles and salads, as well as small informal bistros, mostly in St Peter's Street. **Marlowe's** (No 55) serves steaks, Mexican dishes, vegetarian dishes and salads. **Stowaway's Oyster Bar** (No 53) is a tiny restaurant with a pleasant garden serving a huge range of fish and shellfish. Almost opposite, the **Kentish Cricketers** serves typical English pub food. **Caesar's** (No 46) is a good choice if you have

Resting on the Roman Wall

children, specialising in beefburgers and vegetarian food.

There is more seafood at **Rowland's Bistro** (no 24) and imaginative pub food (for example, rabbit and bacon pie) at the **Three Compasses** (No 18). At No 34, **Teapot** is a characterful teashop serving at least thirty different types of tea and furnished with shelves full of Victorian teapots, whilst **Mother Earth** upstairs serves imaginative vegetarian dishes.

For more formal eating, **George's Brasserie**, 72 George Street, serves crepes and good French/Italian food, and there are two good hotel restaurants: **Sulley's** at the County Hotel and the **Pilgrim Hotel's Carvery**.

Options

Chilham Castle: Castle, gardens, birds of prey and tea rooms (open Easter to mid-October, daily 11am–5pm).

From Canterbury take the A28 Ashford road; after 7 miles/11km, at Bagham, turn right on the A252 and turn left, after 1 mile/1.6km, to **Chilham Castle**.

The castle occupies a splendid hilltop position overlooking the Great Stour river and with a good view back to Canterbury. Much of the original Norman castle was pulled down (though

Chilham Castle gardens

the keep still survives) to be replaced with the graceful red-brick Jacobean mansion (built in 1616) that stands on the site today. Immediately around the house is a series of terraces laid out by the 17th-century gardener and plant collector, John Tradescant, and the park below, with its huge lake, was landscaped by Capability Brown in the 18th century.

Sculpture in Chilham Castle gardens

Eagles, hawks, falcons and owls are bred at the castle and flying displays are given at 3.30pm on Sunday, and Tuesday to Thursday. The tea rooms are located in the Jacobean kitchens of the castle. Chilham village is worth exploring; St Mary's church has excellent funerary monuments by the likes of Inigo Jones and Nicholas Stone.

Goodnestone Park: A must for garden lovers (April to September, Monday to Friday 11am–5pm, Sunday 2–6pm; Tel: 0304-840218 to double check).

From Canterbury take the A257 Sandwich road for 8 miles/12km to Wingham; turn right onto the B2046, take the second left after 1 mile/1.6km and follow the narrow lane for 1 mile/1.6km to **Goodnestone** (pronounced 'Gunston') **Park**. The grounds contain a superb 18th-century walled garden full of old roses, climbing plants, shrubs and perennials, and more old roses grow along the terraces that overlook extensive parkland. The woodland garden and rockery survive as planted in the 1920s and many unusual plants can be bought or ordered at the nursery.

Faversham: Historic town with a wealth of attractive buildings.

From Canterbury drive straight to Faversham along the A2 (12 miles/20km). **Faversham** is one of the most architecturally rewarding towns in England and the best way to explore it is to head for the **Fleur de Lis Heritage Centre** in Preston Street (Monday to Saturday, 9.30am–1pm and 2–4.30pm, closed Thursday and Sunday) and watch the audio-visual presentation before picking up town-trail leaflets.

Do not miss **St Mary's** church with its lovely steeple (built 1799), its carved misericords and 14th-century wall paintings on the Life of Christ. Apart from the Market Place, the most rewarding buildings are in Abbey Street; Thomas Arden, the mayor, was murdered by his wife and her lover in 1550 and the story inspired the famous play, *Arden of Faversham*, which some scholars attribute to Shakespeare, others to Christopher Marlowe.

Goodnestone Park

DAY 2

The North Downs

The highlights of today's journey, from Canterbury to Sevenoaks, are two magnificent palaces: Leeds Castle and Knole.

Leave Canterbury on the A28 Ashford road; after 7 miles/11km, at Bagham, turn right on the A252. You soon pass through Chilham

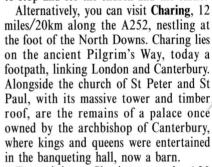

(see *Day 1 Options*) where you may want to stop and see the church and the castle.

Alternatively, you can visit **Charing**, 12 miles/20km along the A252, nestling at the foot of the North Downs. Charing lies on the ancient Pilgrim's Way, today a footpath, linking London and Canterbury. Alongside the church of St Peter and St Paul, with its massive tower and timber roof, are the remains of a palace once owned by the archbishop of Canterbury, where kings and queens were entertained in the banqueting hall, now a barn.

Turn right at Charing onto the A20 Maidstone road; after 10 miles/16km look for the signs to **Leeds Castle** on the left (April to October, daily 11am–5pm; rest of year, Saturday and Sunday 11am–4pm). From the car park there is a walk of nearly 1 mile (1.6 km) to the castle through woodlands and beside a stream.

Leeds Castle and moat

Knole, a 17th-century palace

Leeds Castle is everyone's idea of a fairy-tale castle; it sits on two islands linked by a bridge in the centre of a placid lake, surrounded by a huge expanse of parkland and woods. Leeds is one of England's most ancient castles, named after Led, chief minister of King Ethelbert in AD857. It was rebuilt by the Normans and, from 1272, used as a royal palace – Edward I made it over to his queen, Eleanor, and for the next 300 years it formed part of the dowry which each monarch gave to his queen; hence it is sometimes also known as the 'Lady's Castle'.

The medieval appearance of the castle is, in fact, the result of much later work. It was acquired in 1632 by Sir Thomas Colepeper and his descendant, Fiennes Wykeham-Martin, constructed the main building in 1821 adding the turrets and battlements which lend the castle so much of its charm. In 1925 Lady Baillie purchased the castle and over the next fifty years it was restored to its present state. She started the large collection of waterfowl, including black swans. Other highlights include the **Culpeper Garden**, laid out in 1980 by Russell Page and filled with cottage garden plants; the modern aviaries used for breeding rare and endangered

Deer in the parkland surroundings

The courtyard at Knole

species from all over the world; and the delightful woodland walks where you can escape the crowds and enjoy fine vistas of the castle and lake. At the Fairfax Hall restaurant, you can sample wine from the vineyard, replanted in 1980, nine centuries after Bishop Odo of Bayeux first cultivated grapes on the site.

From Leeds Castle the fastest route to Sevenoaks is to turn left onto the A20 and take the M20 motorway after 1 mile/1.6km. Follow the M20 for 12 miles/20km, then the M26 for 8 miles/13km until it joins the M25 at junction 5. Come off here and follow the signs along the A25 for 3 miles/5km to **Sevenoaks**. Drive through town on the A225 until you see the entrance to **Knole** on the left (house, Easter to end October, Wednesday to Saturday, 11am–5pm, Sunday 2–5pm; park, daily all year to pedestrians).

'A spot compact and mapped out; a maze; a town, yet girt about with walls.' Thus Virginia Woolf described Knole in *Orlando*, her romantic portrait of Vita Sackville-West who is portrayed as the embodiment of all Knole's inhabitants. 'A town' is precise, because the house is vast; count the number of chimneys as you wander around the deer park, to get a rough idea of the number of rooms.

Knole was begun in 1456 by Thomas Bourchier, Archbishop of Canterbury, and greatly extended after 1603 when Elizabeth I gave

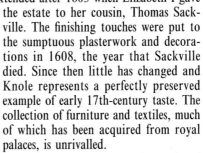

the estate to her cousin, Thomas Sackville. The finishing touches were put to the sumptuous plasterwork and decorations in 1608, the year that Sackville died. Since then little has changed and Knole represents a perfectly preserved example of early 17th-century taste. The collection of furniture and textiles, much of which has been acquired from royal palaces, is unrivalled.

It is well worth buying the National Trust guidebook to help you understand all that is displayed. Ask room attendants to light up details of the gorgeously coloured needlework upholstery with their torches; the rooms are deliberately darkened to ensure that sunlight does not fade the precious textiles.

After exploring the house, return to Sevenoaks and take a walk up the attractive High Street in order to enjoy the many fine 17th- and 18th-century houses before you head for your overnight accommodation.

In the grounds of Leeds Castle

Tourist Information/ Accommodation Booking Service

Sevenoaks Library
Buckhurst Lane
Sevenoaks
Tel: 0732-453118
Open daily 10am–5pm except Sunday.

Accommodation

THE FRIARS
Aylesford
Nr Maidstone
Tel: 0622-717272
If your taste runs to something a little out of the ordinary, try booking a room in this unique former Carmelite monastery just north of Maidstone and within easy reach of the town of Sevenoaks by motorway. The rooms are plain but very comfortable, there is no no bar or TV but warm hospitality and delightful, tranquil surroundings are guaranteed; prices are very low and children are welcome.

Sevenoaks High Street

DONNINGTON MANOR
London Road
Dunton Green
Tel: 0732-462681
Just north of Sevenoaks, in delightful Wealden countryside, with restaurant. Moderate to expensive.

ROYAL OAK
Upper High Street
Sevenoaks
Tel: 0732-451109
Refurbished Georgian coaching inn in attractive, central location close to the entrance to Knole and opposite the 18th-century buildings of Sevenoaks School. Expensive.

SEVENOAKS PARK
Seal Hallow Road
Sevenoaks
Tel: 0732-454245
Set in large gardens with heated outdoor pool. Moderate to expensive.

Eating Out

BLIGHS
135 High Street
Sevenoaks
Tel: 0732-454092
The Carvery of this heavily timbered former farmhouse serves ample helpings of roast meats and vegetarian dishes. A good choice if you are travelling with children.

CASA D'OR
115 London Road
Sevenoaks
Tel: 0732-458282
Choose between the restaurant serving seafood, steaks and Italian-

30

influenced dishes, or the less expensive bistro for lighter meals and vegetarian food.

CHEQUERS
High Street
Sevenoaks
Tel: 0732-454377
Sixteenth-century coaching inn at the crossroads which marks the centre of the town; authentic pub atmosphere and hearty pub food.

GRACELAND PALACE
65 London Road
Sevenoaks
Tel: 0732-455600
Peking, Szechuan and Cantonese dishes. The owner, Hong Kong-born Paul Chan, entertains guests by singing Presley songs at weekends.

SUN DO
61 High Street
Sevenoaks
Tel: 0732-453299
Up-market and expensive Cantonese restaurant.

Ightham Mote

Options

Ightham Mote: The most complete and unspoiled moated manor house in England (open Easter to end October, Monday, Wednesday, Thursday, Friday noon–5.30pm, Sunday 11am–5.30pm). Afternoon tour.

From Sevenoaks take the A25 Ightham road for 4 miles/6km; turn right down a lane signposted to Ivy Hatch and look for National Trust signs for **Ightham Mote** in the village. This 14th-century manor house lies down a narrow lane and is surrounded by a moat (mote in Norman French). You are quite likely to fall in love with it, and you could have bought it had you been around in 1951 when it was last sold. Fortunately the philanthropic American purchaser bequeathed it to the National Trust, which has now begun major restoration work.

Sensibly, the Trust decided not to close the house while restoration took place, but to let the public see the work in progress. You can watch master craftsmen repairing ancient timber beams or consolidating medieval plaster. The lovely gardens have also been replanted and are improving every year.

Chartwell and Westerham: Visit the former homes of two military heroes – Sir Winston Churchill and General Wolfe, then stop at a garden with sweeping views. Afternoon tour.

From Sevenoaks drive along the A25 Reigate road; after 5 miles/8km, just before Westerham, turn left on the B2026 and take

Chartwell, where Churchill lived

the third left after 2 miles/3km to **Chartwell** (Easter to end October, Tuesday to Thursday noon–5.30pm, Saturday and Sunday 11am–5.30pm). Churchill's former home is one of the most-visited sights in the country and you may have to wait some time to get inside (you will be given a numbered, timed ticket on arrival). For many, the real attraction of Chartwell is the terraced garden, laid out by Lady Churchill, the lake with its black swans and Sir Winston's paintings, displayed in the garden studio where he worked.

Return to **Westerham** with its broad green, lined with 18th-century houses. Statues commemorate Churchill and another local hero, General Wolfe, who spent his early years at **Quebec House** (Easter to end October, daily except Thursday and Saturday, 2–6pm). The 17th-century house has material relating to his career and displays on the Battle of Quebec.

Quebec House

At the other end of Westerham is **Squerryes Court** (open April to September, Wednesday, Saturday and Sunday 2–6pm), a fine William and Mary manor house. This contains more Wolfe momentoes but, again, it is the gardens, lake and homemade teas that make a visit worthwhile.

On the way back to Sevenoaks along the A25, turn right in Sundridge (3 miles/5km east of Westerham) and drive towards Ide Hill. After 3 miles/5km, look for the signs to **Emmetts Garden** on the right (open Wednesday to Sunday, 2–5pm). Here you will find a hillside garden planted with unusual trees and shrubs, and enthralling views over the Weald.

The High Weald

This tour takes you through some of the most beautiful country-side and towns in Kent, to the Whitbread Hop Farm and to the world-famous gardens at Sissinghurst. In the afternoon you visit the delightful Scotney Castle gardens and then head for the elegant spa town of Tunbridge Wells.

From Sevenoaks, take the A25 west for 1 mile/1.6km to join the A21 Tunbridge/Hastings road southbound. After 13 miles/20km, take the first exit left to Pembury and follow signs for the B2015.

As you drive, you will see some of the characteristic features of the Weald, a Saxon word meaning wooded country. Rolling hills are covered in dense tracts of oak, chestnut, hornbeam, ash and birch. Timber from the Weald was once used for shipbuilding and charcoal production – a major source of fuel for iron-smelting, another of the region's ancient industries.

Chestnut was used to build the heavily timbered farmhouses and local clay for the rust-red peg tiles that cover the sweeping roofs of many local houses. Many farms also have noble barns and clusters of tall conical oast houses, whose white cowls once turned with the wind and drew air up through the oast to dry the hop flowers. Today most of the oasts are redundant, many of them converted to dwellings, but this morning we will visit one of the last surviving hop farms in Kent.

Carry on along the B2015 for 8 miles/13km, through Whetsted,

Oast houses at Whitbread Hop Farm

Worker on the hop farm

to the junction with the B2160; turn left and shortly after, at Beltring, look for the **Whitbread Hop Farm** on the left (open April to November, 10am–5pm). The Victorian oast houses contain an exhibition telling the story of hops and beer-making, and of the annual summer migration, when families from the East End of London came to Kent to earn money picking hops and have a holiday in the countryside. Here too you can admire beautiful shire horses, bred to pull the brewers' drays which Whitbread still uses for delivering beer from its London brewery.

From the roundabout at the exit to the hop farm, take the B2160 Paddock Wood Road for 8 miles/13 km to another roundabout where you turn right to rejoin the A21 Hastings road. After 6 miles/10km, turn left on the A262 and continue for 4 miles/6km to **Goudhurst** (car park to the right at the crossroads).

Goudhurst is splendidly sited on the top of a hill, 400ft/122m above sea level with extensive views over the surrounding woodland, plus picturesque houses displaying the major characteristics of Wealden architecture. Some are tile-hung, others weatherboarded in a style that had a considerable effect on American colonial architecture when many Wealden carpenters sought a better life in the New World. The church of St Mary dominates the main street and is worth visiting for its brasses and monuments.

Continue on the A262 for 5 miles/8km to the A229 junction. Here you have a choice. The **Granary Restaurant** at **Sissinghurst Castle** opens at noon (though the gardens do not open until 1pm on weekdays) so you could head straight there for an early lunch, along the A262 for another 2miles/3km until you turn left for the castle, just past Sissinghurst village. Or turn left on the A229 and after 5 miles/8km, just before Staplehurst, turn right on the Frit-

One of the first beer delivery vans

A typical house in Goudhurst

tenden road then right again to reach **Iden Croft Herb Garden** (open Monday to Saturday, 9am–5pm, Sunday 11am–5pm).

Although this is a major commercial enterprise, supplying fresh herbs to the catering trade, it has been laid out as a delightfully romantic garden, with over 600 varieties of plants lending their fragrance to the air as you wander along the grass paths.

Retrace your steps to **Sissinghurst Castle** (open April to mid-October, Tuesday to Friday 1–6.30pm, Saturday and Sunday 10–4.30pm). Vita Sackville-West moved here, with her husband, Harold Nicolson, in 1930, after growing up at Knole. It did not matter that the castle was in ruins and the grounds filled with mounds of rubble: Vita set about making what has become the most famous garden in the world, aided by an army of gardeners and by Harold, who was responsible for the plan.

In spring, the bulb garden is a blaze of colour and contains many unusual plants that Vita collected when she rode across Turkey and Iran to visit Harold who was working at the British Embassy in Tehran. From spring on, the climbing plants, the roses and the perennials bloom in

Sissinghurst Castle

profusion, and the White Garden is at its best when the roses covering the central arches are in full flower in late June to early July. For a different perspective, climb the tower and look down on the garden laid out below.

If you can drag yourself away, retrace your steps along the A262 through Goudhurst and turn left on the A21, passing through

Picnic in the grounds of Sissinghurst Castle

Lamberhurst; at the top of the long hill that climbs out of Lamberhurst, look for an easily missed left turn, on a bend, signposted to **Scotney Castle** (open April to mid-November, Wednesday to Friday 11am–6pm, Saturday and Sunday 2–6pm).

The Elizabethan-style house you see from the car park was built in 1843 and deliberately sited to command the best views of the Bewel Valley below, where the remains of the 14th-century castle stand, romantically reflected in the lake. Stone for the upper house was quarried from the hillside and the quarry is now an intriguing garden where plants cling precariously to the rock face.

Leaving Scotney, turn right on the A21, and almost immediately left on the B2169 Tunbridge Wells road into **Lamberhurst.** Just after the turning you will pass the Brown Trout, renowned for its inexpensive fish and seafood dishes. Cross the village green with Priory Vineyards on the right, award-winning producers of English wines. From here you can either head straight to Tunbridge Wells or linger along the route. Garden lovers will enjoy the **Owl House** (first right off the B2169, first right again after 1 mile/1.6km and then left after 1 mile/1.6km; daily 11am–6pm).

A little further along the B2169, on the right, is **Bayham Abbey** (open Easter to end September daily, 10am–6pm). The ruins of this Premonstratensian abbey, founded around 1208, stand to an impressive height and are all the more attractive for their setting amidst the quiet meadows along the River Teise. Continue along the leafy B2169 and the next turn left leads to **Bartley Mill**, once owned by the Bayham Abbey estate (daily 10am–6pm). The water mill now produces flour from organic wheat grown on the surrounding farm; you can watch the milling process, visit the farm museum and walk along the banks of the stream; the mill serves excellent homemade teas and offers bed and breakfast accommodation, making it an excellent base for exploring the area.

Tourist Information/ Accommodation Booking Service

Monson House
Monson Way
Tunbridge Wells
Tel: 0892-515675
Open daily 9.30am–5pm except for Sunday.

Accommodation

Bartley Mill
Bells Yew Green, Frant
Tel: 0892-890372
Delightful water mill 5 miles/8km southeast of Tunbridge Wells; bed and breakfast in the farmhouse, home-made food. Inexpensive.

Calverley Hotel
Crescent Road
Tunbridge Wells
Tel: 0892-26455
Former summer residence of the Duchess of Kent, mother of Queen Victoria, now an elegant hotel. Moderate to expensive.

Kingswood
Pembury Road
Tunbridge Wells
Tel: 0892-35736
Edwardian house with fine woodwork and quiet gardens, plus stylish rooms and home-cooked food. Moderate to expensive.

Russell
80, London Road
Tunbridge Wells
Tel: 0892-544833
Friendly small hotel on the common, minutes from the centre. Moderate to expensive.

Spa
Mount Ephraim
Tunbridge Wells
Tel: 0892-20331

Elegant mansion built in 1766, beautifully furnished and redolent of Regency England. It also has modern facilities such as an indoor pool, gym and a tennis court. Expensive.

Swan
The Pantiles
Tunbridge Wells
Tel: 0892-541450
Recently restored 17th-century coaching inn located in the Pantiles and therefore right on the spot for the town's best shops and pavement cafés. Moderate to expensive.

Vale Royal
54/57 London Road
Tunbridge Wells
Tel: 0892-25580
The best rooms here overlook the hotel's charming rose-filled gardens. Moderate.

Eating Out

Cheevers
56 High Street
Tunbridge Wells
Tel: 0892-545324
Imaginative French-influenced cuisine.

Davinci
46 High Street
Tunbridge Wells

Tel: 0892-24857
Wine bar, restaurant and nightclub serving English and Continental food.

EGLANTINE
65 High Street
Tunbridge Wells
Tel: 0892-24957
Nouvelle Cuisine and the best vegetarian dishes in town.

GRACELAND PALACE
3 Cumberland Walk
Tunbridge Wells
Tel: 0892-540754
Between the High Street and the Pantiles. Peking, Szechuan and Cantonese dishes.

KENDALS at the **SWAN HOTEL**
The Pantiles
Tunbridge Wells
Tel: 0892-541450
Good seafood.

RUPERT'S CAFE
30 High Street
Tunbridge Wells
Tel: 0892-511045
Young-ish haunt serving American-style beefburgers and pasta.

XIAN
54 High Street
Tunbridge Wells
Tel: 0892-22930
Top quality Szechuan cuisine.

Options

Tunbridge Wells: A morning tour of the shops and historic buildings of this famous spa town.

Tunbridge Wells used to be a by-word for refined gentility but it has become a busy, young and prosperous town, the shopping centre for much of West Kent and East Sussex. It sits on a hill and is divided into two; the upper town is brash, busy and modern and, in the pedestrianised Calverley Road precinct, you will find all the major UK chain-store retailers. The lower town, from the railway station down to the Pantiles, is the most interesting. Its High Street is lined with tea shops, wine bars and shops selling books,

The Pantiles in Tunbridge Wells

antiques, clothes and furnishings.

To explore the lower town, park in the Clarence Road multi-storey car park, next to the station. Head down the High Street to the Pantiles. The history of this elegant colonnaded street is essentially the history of Tunbridge Wells. In 1606 the town did not exist and the area was covered in the dense woodland of Waterdown Forest. The chalybeate (iron-bearing) spring was discovered by Lord North while out hunting. He developed its commercial potential and soon kings, queens and courtiers were coming to enjoy its healing waters. The buildings of the Pantiles were begun in the late 17th century and the rest of the town, with its parks, crescents and fine early Victorian architecture, was laid out from 1830 onwards.

The Pantiles is named after the original paving material used but only 15 of the original terracotta pantiles survive, located near the Bathhouse. Principal buildings are the **Bathhouse**, with its spring, on the right as you enter the street, and the **Corn Exchange**, half-

Corn Exchange in Tunbridge Wells

way up on the left. Originally built as a theatre, it houses a shopping mall and a series of tableaux illustrating the town's history, called *A Day at the Wells* (1 April to 31 October daily 9.30am–5.30pm; 1 November to 31 March daily, 10am–4pm). There are numerous pavement cafés where in summer you can watch buskers and outdoor entertainment.

As you leave the Pantiles, cross the road to the red-brick church of **King Charles the Martyr**. This rare dedication to the executed Charles I shows that Tunbridge Wells was staunchly Royalist when the church was built in the 1680s. Lunchtime concerts and organ recitals are given here on Thursday and Saturday throughout the summer.

Chapel Place, behind the church, has the best concentration of intriguing small shops – antiques and second-hand books spill out onto the pavement to tempt browsers. Wine bars and cafés beckon as you climb back up the hill. At the top, behind the rather ugly 1930s Town Hall and theatre, is the town **Museum and Art Gallery**

Hever Castle

(Monday to Saturday, 9.30am–5pm), housing a collection of Tunbridge Ware, decorative boxes and novelties made locally since the 18th century, as well as local archaeological material.

Hever, Chiddingstone and Penshurst:
An afternoon taking in two of England's oldest and most appealing stately homes.

From Tunbridge Wells take the A246 East Grinstead Road; after 10 miles/16km turn right on the B2026. Take the second right after 4 miles/6km; after 1 mile/1.6km, in Markbeech, turn left and drive for 2 miles/3km to **Hever** village. The **castle** (daily April to October, 11am–5pm), stands four-square and immaculate in the centre of its mirror-like moat, little changed externally since the 13th and 14th centuries. In 1462 it was bought by the Bullen (or Boleyn) family; Anne Boleyn, second wife of Henry VIII and mother of Elizabeth I, was born here and the Long Gallery features an exhibition on her life and times. William Waldorf Astor acquired the estate in 1903. He was responsible for the castle's superb Edwardian woodcarving and plasterwork, for building up its rich collection of paintings and furniture and creating

Church in Chiddingstone

In the gardens of Penshurst Place

the outstanding gardens with their Roman and Renaissance sculpture, cascades and fountains.

You can lunch at Hever Castle or at the Henry VIII inn in the village. The Kentish Horse pub in Markbeech is also excellent. Best of all, especially for its picturesque setting, is the **Castle Inn** in **Chiddingstone**. Turn right out of the castle grounds and take the next three right turns. After 3 miles/5km you cross the pretty River Eden, then turn left into Chiddingstone, a delightful village of 16th- and 17th-century timber-framed houses.

After lunch, head for **Penshurst**; continue through Chiddingstone, turn left and drive for 1 mile/1.6km to the B2027 where you turn right. After 1 mile/1.6km, just after Penshurst station, turn right on the B2176 and, after 3 miles/5km is the entrance to **Penshurst Place** (daily April to September, 12.30–5.30pm).

Standing beside the River Medway, surrounded by neat estate cottages and cow-filled meadows, Penshurst would still be recognisable to Ben Johnson, who, in the early 17th century, wrote a poem in praise of the house and its owners, the Sidney family, in which he mentions 'Thy Mount, to which the dryads do resort'.

You may not see any dryads but the Mount is still there at the centre of a formal garden laid out as it was when Johnson wrote his poem. The whole of the gardens are a delight, ranging from the simplicity of the Nut Garden, planted with Kentish cobs (hazelnuts) to the colourful complexity of the flower and shrub borders.

Inside, the impressive Great Hall is the earliest surviving example in England of a medieval hall with central fireplace. Some 60ft/18m high, the hall had no chimney: the smoke simply dispersed in the room. Other rooms are more gorgeously furnished, with an outstanding series of Sidney family portraits, (including that of the Elizabethan poet Sir Philip Sidney, who was born in the house). To return to Tunbridge Wells, turn left out of Penshurst onto the B2176, then turn right, after 5 miles/8km, on the A26.

Wakehurst Place

Ashdown Forest

Once a vast and impenetrable royal hunting ground, Ashdown Forest has been tamed by man. Today you will visit two large gardens carved out of the forest, Wakehurst Place and Sheffield Park, and take a ride on the Bluebell Steam Railway.

As Kipling wrote: 'Our England is a garden and such gardens are not made / By singing "Oh, how beautiful", and sitting in the shade'. No indeed, such gardens are only made by years of toil; and often with the aid of an army of gardeners. That, more than anything else, is perhaps why Southeast England has such a large number of outstanding Edwardian gardens – economic resources counted as much as soil, which is, in any case, rather infertile here. Early 20th-century Sussex was prosperous and populated by people rich enough to patronise the pioneers of modern gardening – the likes of William Robinson, whose wild and informal style of planting was developed at Gravetye Manor near East Grinstead, and Gertrude Jekyll, queen of the herbaceous border, who gardened at Munstead Wood near Godalming.

Today, few individuals can command the resources to maintain gardens on the grand scale and it is only through the work of in-

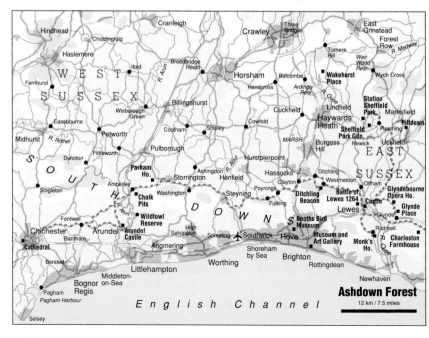

Ashdown Forest

12 km / 7.5 miles

stitutions, such as the Royal Botanic Gardens at Kew, and the National Trust, that the most grandiose gardens survive. You will visit two today. First, to Wakehurst Place. Take the A264 from Tunbridge Wells to East Grinstead (14 miles/22km), then the B2110 to Turners Hill (6 miles/10km), where you turn left on the B2028. **Wakehurst Place** is on the right after 4 miles/6km (daily from 10am).

The construction of the garden was begun at the beginning of the century by Lord Wakehurst who planted the now-mature and magnificent collection of trees and shrubs from all over the world. Since the staff of the Royal Botanic Gardens at Kew took over the management in 1965, the garden has been enhanced by the creation of a Himalayan glade, water gardens around the man-made Westwood Lake and rock gardens laid among the naturally occurring sandstone outcrops.

After wandering along the wooded slopes and discovering new vistas and interesting plants, you can have lunch in the 16th-century house before heading for **Sheffield Park**. Turn right and take

Bluebell Railway locomotives

the B2028 to Lindfield, then take a left turn along the B2111 for 2 miles/3km to join the A272. Turn left and, after 4 miles/6km, left again on the A275. Sheffield Park station can then be found on the left, after 3 miles/5km.

Here you can explore the locomotive sheds and the museum, whose exhibits explain the history of this most delightful of steam railways, which is kept alive by enthusiastic volunteers. Climb aboard one of the trains that run at roughly hourly intervals along the **Bluebell Railway** from the end of May to the end of September, less frequently during the rest of the year. The train chugs up the gradient to the Victorian station at Horsted Keynes, a 15-minute journey that recreates the romance of the great days of steam, then back through the lovely wooded countryside, carpeted with bluebells in early summer.

Next you head for Sheffield Park **gardens**; left on the A275 and the entrance is on the right after 1 mile/1.6km (April to mid-November, Tuesday to Saturday, 11am–6pm and Sunday 2–6pm). Capability Brown laid out the basic structure in 1775; to his lower lakes, two upper lakes and a linking cascade were added in the

Thundery evening near Sheffield Park

19th century. Massed planting of trees and shrubs took place from 1909 onwards, designed to ensure that the shapes and colours are fully appreciated from carefully sited viewpoints. Buy a garden map at the entrance and follow one of the delightful recommended walks.

When you leave Sheffield Park it is worth calling at **Fletchling** (right on the A275, first right shortly afterwards down a narrow lane, then take the next two right turns until you reach the village after 3 miles/5km). The Norman church of St Mary and St Andrew contains interesting monuments, including the mausoleum of Edward Gibbon, author of *The Decline and Fall of the Roman Empire*. Turn left by the church and follow the lane to **Piltdown**, now a golf course, where the skull of 'Piltdown Man' was discovered in 1912. Hailed for years as the missing link in the evolutionary chain between man and ape it was exposed as a hoax in the 1950s. Cross the A272 and follow the signs to Isfield, with its Norman church standing beside a tributary of the River Ouse. Beyond Isfield the lane joins the A26, from where it is just 5 miles/8km to Lewes.

If time permits, bypass Lewes and turn eastwards onto the A27; within 5 miles/8km of the junction lie two more interesting houses: the 16th-century **Glynde Place**, open occasionally during the summer, and **Firle Place** in its surrounding hamlet of West Firle (south of the road), with 16th-century alabaster effigies and several brasses in its church. To the south looms the 712-ft/217-m Firle Beacon and this is a good starting point for a short walk along the South Downs.

A little further to the east along the A27, signs direct you down a lane to the right leading to **Charleston Farmhouse**: here the painter Duncan Grant lived for many years with Vanessa and Clive Bell, and the house is a mecca for enthusiasts of the Bloomsbury Group, most of whom were regular visitors. Recently restored and opened to the public, its rooms are covered

Misty day in Sheffield Park

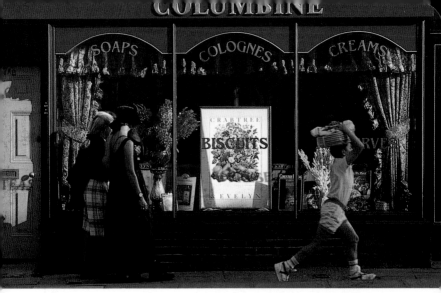

Window shopping on Lewes High Street

with the tenants' paintings and decorations on almost every available surface, and the downstairs studio is preserved exactly as it was when Grant died at an advanced age in 1978. Together, Vanessa Bell and Duncan Grant also laid out the small but charmingly informal garden.

Tourist Information/ Accommodation Booking Service

32 High Street
Lewes
Tel: 0273-483448
Open Easter to end September, Monday to Friday, 9am–5pm, Saturday 10am–1pm. Rest of year Monday to Friday 9am–1pm and 2–5pm.

Lewes makes a better base for exploring the south coast than its bigger, brasher neighbours such as Eastbourne and Brighton.

Accommodation

BARN HOUSE
Rodmell
Near Lewes
Tel: 0273-477865
Converted 17th-century barn near Virginia Woolf's home, 6 miles/10km south of Lewes. Furnished with antiques and strongly recommended as a quiet rural base for exploring the area. Moderate.

BERKELEY HOUSE
1 Albion Street
Lewes
Tel: 0273-476057
An elegant Georgian town house in a quiet centrally situated street. Atmospheric candlelit restaurant. No smoking. Moderate.

MANOR FARM
Ripe,
Near Lewes
Tel: 0323-811425
Elegant manor house offering bed and breakfast in a quiet downland village where Malcolm Lowry once lived, 6 miles/10km east of Lewes. Inexpensive.

MILLERS
134 High Street
Lewes
Tel: 0273-475631
A sixteenth-century timber-framed house with Bloomsbury Group associations. No smoking. Moderate.

RINGMER INN
Lewes Road
Ringmer
Tel: 0273-812438
Vine-covered Victorian inn with luxury rooms and an up-market Chinese restaurant, situated 2 miles/3km east of Lewes. Moderate.

SHELLEY'S
High Street
Lewes
Tel: 0273-472361
A 17th-century house with restaurant overlooking fine gardens. Expensive.

WHITE HART
High Street
Lewes
Tel: 0273-474676
An old coaching inn with traditional oak-beamed bedrooms; a choice of coffee shops and restaurants. Moderate to expensive.

Eating Out

CROWN HOTEL
Market Street
Lewes
Tel: 0273-480670
Inexpensive pub food in a popular and central location.

KENWARD'S
Pipe Passage
Lewes
Tel: 0273-472343
Inventive gourmet-standard dishes. Expensive.

PELHAM ARMS
St Anne's Hill/High Street corner
Lewes
Tel: 0273-476149
Popular pub selling homemade food. No meals Sunday evening.

SEASONS
199 High Street, Lewes
Tel: 0273-473968
Basement restaurant specialising in vegetarian dishes.

THACKERY'S
3 Malling Street
Lewes
Tel: 0273-474634
Candlelit restaurant with a French-influenced menu. Closed Sunday and Monday.

PAILIN THAI RESTAURANT
19/20 Station Street
Lewes
Tel: 0273-433906
Tiny restaurant with a huge menu including vegetarian dishes.

WEIGHED INN
Bear Lane
Lewes
Tel: 0273-477737
Quiet retreat in the lower town offering homemade food.

WHITE HART HOTEL
55 High Street
Lewes
Tel: 0273-474676
Carvery restaurant for formal dining and coffee shop serving snacks and light meals.

Lewes High Street in evening light

Lewes: A town for connoisseurs of English architecture with an imposing castle, good shopping and pubs selling locally brewed Harvey's beer. Morning tour.

The name **Lewes** comes from the Saxon *hlaew*, meaning hill. Of the town's many hills, Castle Hill is the most prominent, and we will head there first for a view of the town and its surroundings. Park in the car park in North Street, turn right up Market Street and right again into the High Street, with its timber and brick houses. On the right is the **castle** entrance (open daily 11am–5pm but closed Sunday, November to March). Alongside is Barbican House, housing an excellent archaeological museum and the castle gatehouse with its 'Lewes Living History' audio-visual display.

Citizen of Lewes

The castle, approached by means of an impressive Barbican and Norman gatehouse, was built by William the Conqueror's right-hand man, William de Warenne, in AD1100. It occupies a strategic position, guarding the Ouse valley; climb the battlements to see the commanding view down the River Ouse to the sea and to the steep escarpments of the South Downs which seem completely to surround the town.

From here turn left down Castle Lane and New Road, then left along the narrow Pipe Passage, which follows the line of the medieval town walls. This takes us back to the High Street and **Bull House**, where Tom Paine lived

47

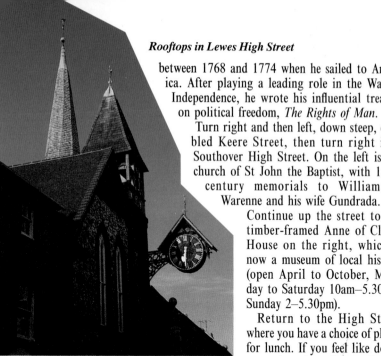

Rooftops in Lewes High Street

between 1768 and 1774 when he sailed to America. After playing a leading role in the War of Independence, he wrote his influential treatise on political freedom, *The Rights of Man*.

Turn right and then left, down steep, cobbled Keere Street, then turn right into Southover High Street. On the left is the church of St John the Baptist, with 12th-century memorials to William de Warenne and his wife Gundrada.

Continue up the street to the timber-framed Anne of Cleves House on the right, which is now a museum of local history (open April to October, Monday to Saturday 10am–5.30pm, Sunday 2–5.30pm).

Return to the High Street where you have a choice of places for lunch. If you feel like doing some shopping afterwards, the High Street offers antique toys, books, imaginative modern jewellery, herbal products, modern paintings and oriental rugs.

Brighton: **A trip to the seaside to see one of England's most exotic buildings – the Royal Pavilion – to stroll along the pier and promenade and shop in the Lanes district. Morning, afternoon or whole day tour.**

It is best to take the train to Brighton; there are frequent services from Lewes station. If you choose to drive, the best place to park is in the car park by the station, then walk down Queen's Road and take the third left into Church Street. Continue until you reach Marlborough Place, and turn right, down Pavilion Parade, to the **Royal Pavilion** (open daily June to September 10am–6pm, rest of year 10am–5pm).

This wonderfully eccentric building, with its minarets and onion domes, was commissioned by the Prince Regent, later King George IV. He visited what was then the fishing village of Brighthelmstone in 1783 and bought a farmhouse, which the architect Henry Holland con-

Lavish flower decorations

verted into a simple, classical villa. But the Prince, inspired by the eastern splendour of Sezincote, a country house in the spa town of Cheltenham, then entrusted John Nash with the task of making his seaside palace more exotic. The result is an eclectic blend of oriental styles, decorated with red and gold dragons, lavish gilding and costly furniture.

If your tastes are for simpler, modern design, turn left back to Church Street, for the **Brighton Museum and Art Gallery** (open Tuesday to Saturday, 10am–5pm, Sunday 2–5pm). This is also in Indian style and was converted in 1873 from the former royal stables. Inside are paintings by Vanessa Bell and Duncan Grant, good examples of art nouveau and art deco design and displays that trace Brighton's transformation from a sleepy fishing village to one of England's most popular holiday resorts.

From the museum walk back past the Pavilion and down Old Steine to emerge by **Palace Pier**. This superb structure, painted white and stretching a quarter of a mile/400m into the sea, was built at the end of the 19th century. Walk its length to enjoy views of the whole seafront, with the new Brighton Marina, to the right.

From the pier turn left and continue along the seafront, then right into East Street and left into the area known as the **Lanes**. This warren of narrow streets represents the surviving core of the old fishing village, and is now given over to fascinating small shops selling books, antiques, crafts, jewellery and works of art. Here, too, you will find pavement cafés for coffee, lunch or tea.

The Royal Pavilion in Brighton

Chichester and Arundel: This is a long day, but a rewarding one, full of variety, that takes us first to the cathedral town of Chichester, then back to Lewes via Denmans Garden, Arundel, with its castle and wetlands nature reserve, Amberley Chalk Pits Museum and Parham House. **Whole day tour.**

From Lewes, avoid the obvious route to Chichester, the south coast road, unless you like traffic jams and suburban sprawl. Take the quieter South Downs route, passing through unspoiled countryside: the A275 north for 3 miles/5km; left after Offham, on the B2116. After 5 miles/8km, at Westmeston, carry straight on to

Brighton pier at sunset

Clayton where you can see St John the Baptist church, renowned for its well-preserved 12th-century wall paintings.

In Clayton turn left on the A273 and right, after 2 miles/3km onto the A281. When this road bends sharply to the right, after 3 miles/5km, carry straight on along the lane that passes through the villages of Poynings and Fulking; the Downs to your left are a favourite launch-pad for hang-gliders. Turn left on the A2037, through Upper Beeding, and right on the A283 through Bamber, Steyning and Washington to Storrington. Turn left here, on the B2139, through Houghton, then follow the A29/27 to **Chichester**.

Complex as it sounds, this is an attractive drive and easy to follow. It brings you to the Chichester ring road where you follow signs to the town centre and Festival Theatre. Park in the car park beside the theatre and take the subway walk under the roundabout to emerge in North Street. Follow this to the heart of town, marked by the ornate Market Cross, built in 1501. The Roman town of Noviomagus (New Market) became the Saxon Cissa's Ceastre (Cissa's Camp), then medieval Chichester, but the market has remained the focal point of the town for two millenia, located where the four original Roman streets intersect.

Arundel Cathedral

Turn right in West Street to find the **cathedral** entrance and spend the next hour or so exploring this rewarding Norman and Early English church. Gorgeous colours draw the eye, provided by John Piper's fiery altar-screen tapestry and Marc Chagall's *Creation* stained-glass window. Don't miss two outstanding Romanesque (mid 12th-cen-

50

Clocktower in Chichester

tury) carved panels depicting the Raising of Lazarus and the Miracle at Bethany. These dramatic and well-preserved reliefs are among the best of their date in Europe. Equally engaging are the passageways of the cathedral close and views of the cathedral from the Bishop's Palace Gardens.

Chichester has two good lunch spots. **Micawbers**, 13 South Street (Tel: 0243 786989) is a restaurant with French character specialising in fresh shellfish and seafood; try the superb *fruits de mer*. **Sadlers** wine bar and restaurant, 42 East Street (Tel: 0243 774765) serves steaks, fish and poultry.

Leave Chichester on the A27 Arundel Road and drive for 6 miles/10km to Fontwell. Continue past the racecourse, ignore the A29 turning but take the next right and immediately left, down Denmans Lane, to reach **Denmans Garden** (open 5 March to 16 December 9am–5pm daily). One of the best modern gardens in England, planted since 1946, and an inspiration to all gardeners who are struggling to create Eden out of a wilderness. The exuberant planting guarantees that there is something new round every corner and the garden is well complemented by the buildings of the Clock House, where landscape designer John Brookes runs the School of Garden Design.

From Denmans go back to the A27, turn right and continue on to Arundel, another 5 miles/8km. Arundel is a deceptive place. It looks French and medieval, with its hilltop castle and spiky Gothic cathedral, but the cathedral was built in 1873 and the castle between 1890 and 1903, on the site of its Norman predecessor. The castle is well worth visiting for its sheer Victorian exuberance, and

The towers of Arundel Castle

a good collection of portraits of the Dukes of Norfolk, whose seat this is (open April to October, daily except Saturday, 1–5pm).

Compared to the Gothicism of the cathedral, I prefer the humbler parish church of **St Nicholas**, just down from the castle. It is uniquely divided: physically by a glass screen and doctrinally by the fact that the chancel is reserved for the use of the castle's owners, the Roman Catholic Dukes of Norfolk, while the nave is the preserve of Arundel's Anglican parishioners.

The best-views of Arundel are from **Burpham**, on the other side of the valley, or from the Wildfowl Trust in Mill Road, which runs along beside the river below the castle and past Swanbourne Lake (daily 9.30am–6.30pm in summer, 9.30am–5pm in winter). The centre was founded by the naturalist Peter Scott on 60 acres/24ha of wetlands bordering the River Arun. Paths crisscross between ponds and reed-beds to hides where you can watch rare wildfowl, both the many permanent residents of the reserve and, at the right times of year, passing migrants.

Leave Arundel on the A284 and turn right on the B2139 after 4 miles/6km. Just after you pass Amberley railway station, turn right for the **Chalk Pits Museum** (daily 17 July to 8 September, 10am–6pm, otherwise, 20 March to 27 October, Wednesday to Saturday 10am–6pm). This award-winning open-air museum covers the industrial archaeology of southeast England. You can watch craftsmen working and take a ride on a narrow-gauge railway. Children love Amberley, but if you prefer stately houses and gardens, carry on to the next destination.

Continue along the B2139 to Storrington, turn left on the A283 and left again, after 1 mile/1.6km, to **Parham House** (Easter to October Sunday, Wednesday and Thursday 2–6pm). Highlights of this fine Tudor house include one of the most famous portraits of Elizabeth I (by Zucchero), and a superb collection of 16th- and 17th-century embroidery. Parham also has extensive and beautifully laid-out gardens. To return to Lewes, simply follow this morning's route in reverse.

Street scenery in Arundel

The South Downs

A day spent exploring the nature reserves and country parks of the South Downs around Alfriston. Blow the cobwebs away with a good stiff walk.

From Lewes take the A27 Eastbourne road, which runs parallel to the South Downs. Narrow lanes run off to the right to a series of pretty downland villages, nestling in the sheltered lee of the Downs. After 12 miles/20km, watch out for a sign to Berwick and drive to the peaceful little church of **St Michael and All Angels**.

In the churchyard is a simple headstone marking the grave of Vanessa Bell, who lived at nearby Charleston (see *Day 4*). The walls of the church are covered with paintings by Vanessa and Quentin Bell and Duncan Grant, commissioned by Bishop Bell of Chichester who was keen to promote modern art in churches. But the fact that Grant and the Bells had little sympathy for religious subjects shows; the only work which captures their usual vibrancy is the pulpit, painted with fruit and flowers by Duncan Grant in 1962, after most of Vanessa Bell's original panels had been destroyed by vandals.

Return to the A27 and a short distance on turn right to **Alfriston**. On the left is **Drusilla's Park**, a small zoo with an adventure playground, gardens and family restaurant. Nearby is the English Wine Centre, which sells the products of local vineyards. Alfriston village looks as pretty as a postcard and attracts large numbers of

Surprising splash of colour in Alfriston

Alfriston vicarage

visitors, which makes it a good place for shopping. You will find many shops in the High Street that you would not expect in a small village, selling stylish clothes, art, antiques, pottery and perfumes.

St Andrew's church, known as the Cathedral of the South Downs because of its size, stands in an attractive setting in a bend of the Cuckmere River. Alongside is a domestic building of the same period – the 14th century. The humble **Clergy House** (open Easter to end October daily 11am–6pm) is a typical Wealden-style timber house with an attractive cottage garden, which was the first building to be acquired by the National Trust after its foundation in 1895. The Trust is now responsible for conserving many of England's greatest houses and gardens. There is plenty of choice for lunch in Alfriston, with the **Olde Smugglers Inne**, the **George**, the **Alfriston Wingrove Inn** and the **Sussex Ox** all offering bar and restaurant meals. Or stock up for a picnic at **Ashley's Village Store** in West Street which sells fresh-baked bread and delicatessen foods.

We start our walk by leaving Alfriston on the road you came in on. Take the first right and right again through Litlington to Exceat, pronounced Excete. There used to be a fishing village here, but most of its inhabitants died of the Black Death in the 14th century. Call in at the **Country Park** centre, housed in a traditional Sussex barn, to pick up trail leaflets and see displays on the flora and fauna of this enchanting river valley – the last spot on this

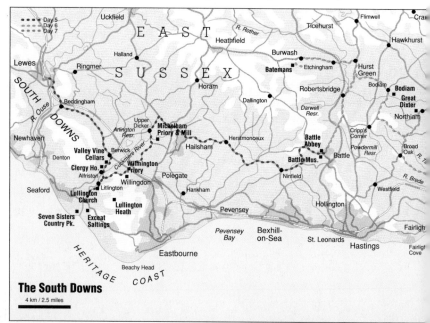

The South Downs

4 km / 2.5 miles

The George Inn in Alfriston

stretch of the coast that was not blighted by unchecked development between the wars. It was partly in response to the despoliation of the South Coast that the Town and Country Planning Act was introduced in 1947, to control development, although many conservationists do not consider this act tough enough.

From Exceat a well-marked path takes you the 2 miles/3km along the meandering Cuckmere to the shingle beach at Cuckmere Haven from where you have a good view of the **Seven Sisters**. This series of sheer chalk cliffs (there are actually eight, but the alliterative Seven Sisters sounds better) is even more dramatic than the better-known White Cliffs of Dover. Retrace your steps to **Litlington**, with its Norman church. If you have any energy left, take the track opposite and climb up to **Lullington Heath National Nature Reserve**, an area of chalk heathland dotted with prehistoric burial mounds and medieval field systems. The village is famous for the **Litlington Tea House**, with its secluded Pleasure Gardens, where you will be served by costumed waitresses. Although you may prefer to wait until Michelham Priory before you stop for tea.

To reach Michelham Priory, continue through Litlington and take the next right; soon you will see **Lullington church** on the left, a delightful flint building with a white turret – it has a seating capacity of just 20. Continue to **Wilmington**, another attractive downland village, and see the remains of the Benedictine priory which stand in the grounds of an 18th-century farmhouse, run as an **agricultural museum** (mid-March to mid-October, 11am–5.30pm, Sunday 2–5.30pm, closed Tuesday) displaying farm-

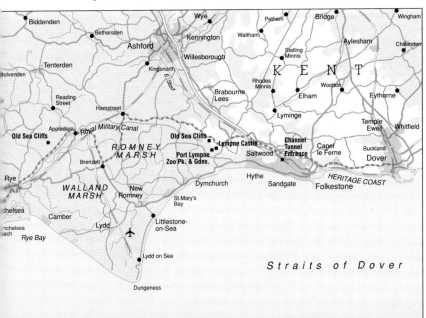

Green gardens in Alfriston

ing implements and household utensils from a bygone era. The grounds offer a good view of the **Long Man of Wilmington**. This enigmatic chalk-cut figure of a giant, striding across the hillside, is first mentioned in documents dating to 1779, so he may not be of any great antiquity, although he could be a prehistoric fertility figure.

Drive through Wilmington, cross the A27 and follow the winding narrow road for 4 miles/6km, finally taking a left turn to reach **Michelham Priory** (25 March to 31 October daily 11am–5.30pm). Tea here consists of bread, scones or cakes made on the premises from flour ground by the Priory's own water mill, driven by the River Cuckmere which forms the Priory's wide moat.

Michelham Priory was founded in the 13th century by the Augustinians and became a farmhouse after the 16th-century Dissolution of the Monasteries. Owned by the Sussex Archaeological Society, it is a beautiful and tranquil spot. Fine gardens surround the Elizabethan wing, which exhibits the work of local artists. Wild-

Cuckmere Valley near Exceat

A penny dropped

fowl swim in the moat and you can explore the mill and a wheelwright's shop as well as an impressive Tudor barn.

When you are ready to move on, turn right and then first right again, through Upper Dicker, where you join the A271. Turn right once more and follow this road for 13 miles/21km through Herstmonceux to Ninfield, then turn left on the A269 and continue for 8 miles/13km on the road that takes you to Battle.

Tourist Information/ Acommodation Booking Service

88 High Street
Battle
Tel: 04246-3721
Open daily 10am–6pm summer, 10am–4pm winter.

Accommodation

GEORGE HOTEL
23 High Street
Battle
Tel: 04246-4466
Comfortable old coaching inn with restaurant and wine bar. Moderate.

LEEFORD PLACE
Mill Lane
Whatlington, Battle
Tel: 04246-62863
Quiet rural retreat, opposite Leeford Vineyards, 2 miles/3km northeast of Battle. Inexpensive.

NETHERFIELD PLACE
Netherfield
Tel: 04246-4455
Georgian country house set in rural surroundings 2 miles/3km north of Battle with a good French restaurant. Expensive.

OLD DEANERY
Upper Lake
Battle
Tel: 04246-4409
A lovely Elizabethan house next to the parish church. This is a quiet, friendly place and very good value. Inexpensive.

POWDERMILLS
Powdermill Lane
Battle
Tel: 04246-5511
Attractive Georgian country house in
extensive grounds 1 mile/1.6km south
west of Battle. Lakes, woods, swim-
ming pool, tennis court and good
food in the Orangery restaurant.
Moderate to expensive.

PRIORY HOSE
17 High Street
Battle
Tel: 04246-3366
Friendly, family-run hotel with
restaurant. Moderate.

Eating Out

BAYEUX
31 Mount Street
Battle
Tel: 04246-2132
French-influenced dishes and vegetar-
ian specialities. Closed Sunday.

BLACKSMITHS
43 High Street
Battle
Tel: 04246-3200
Central European dishes as well as
English and Continental cuisine.
Closed Sunday.

JACK FULLER'S
Brightling
Tel: 042482-212
Excellent pub/restaurant serving inexpensive traditional English food
based on produce from nearby farms,
plus a range of local wines. Difficult
to find so ring for directions. Closed
Monday.

LA VIEILLE AUBERGE
27 High Street
Battle
Tel: 04246-5171
Classic French cuisine. Reservations
advised. Closed Monday and Tuesday.

NETHERFIELD ARMS
Netherfield
Tel: 042482-282
Cosy 16th-century pub serving home-
cooked food and vegetarian dishes.

Entertainment

1066 INN
High Street, Battle
Tel: 04246-3224
Venue for folk evenings every Sunday
at 8pm. Hear some of England's leading performers – traditional and elec-
tric folk. Children welcome, excellent
beer and bar meals.

1066 Country

Today you visit the site of the Battle of Hastings; Bateman's, the house where Rudyard Kipling wrote many of his best-loved works; romantic Bodiam Castle and Great Dixter, the 15th-century home of Christopher Lloyd, the renowned gardener.

Every English schoolchild knows the date 1066; that was the year in which William the Conqueror defeated the Saxon King Harold I at the Battle of Hastings with momentous consequences for the future course of English history. Local people are now fighting another battle: to get the name changed to the Battle of Senlac, since the fighting took place on a ridge called Senlac, where Battle Abbey now stands, and not in Hastings at all.

Main Gate to Battle Abbey

Battle Abbey, whose 1338 gatehouse overlooks the site of the former market place, now a car park, was built on the spot where Harold fell. William founded the abbey to commemorate his victory and the town of Battle grew up around it. Explore the town first, since the abbey does not open until 10am. Park in front of the gatehouse if you can find space, or follow blue signs to the car park alongside the English Heritage Visitor Centre then walk back to the **gatehouse**. From here there is a good view up the High Street, with its raised pavements and tile-hung 18th-century houses and shops. It is worth wandering up the street, browsing in the antique shops, galleries and boutiques.

When you return, continue past the gatehouse to the huge Norman parish church of **St Mary**, with its wall-paintings on the life of St Margaret of Antioch, its brasses and Renaissance monument to Sir Anthony Browne. Look out for the tomb of Isaac Ingall in the churchyard, by the east wall of the chancel; if the inscription is to be believed, he died in 1798 at the ripe old age of 120. The route back to the Abbey passes several antique shops and Buckley's **Museum of Shops**, a unique collection of early packaging and advertising material displayed in a recreation of a Victorian grocer's shop (90 High Street; daily 10am–5.30pm).

Return to the **Battle Abbey Visitor Centre** and, having paid your admission, watch the audio-visual presentation that explains the background to the battle. Afterwards, follow the signs round the battlefield that explain the course of the battle, ending at the spot where Harold died, the site on which the high altar of Battle Abbey was subsequently placed. The battle was small in scale – 7,000 men on each side, fighting over the future of England. Yet the legacy of the victorious Normans remains with us to this day in our language and legal system and the vast number of great cathedrals, churches and castles that they built.

Having toured the abbey and battle site, you may want to take coffee in the **Pilgrim's Rest** restaurant opposite the gatehouse – a fine example of a 15th-century hall house. Leave Battle by

driving up the High Street and follow the A2100, at the roundabout, signposted to London, Mountfield and Sevenoaks. After 4 miles (6.5km) you merge with the busy A21 and follow this for 5 miles (8km) to Hurst Green. Turn left here on the A265 through Etchingham and Burwash (4 miles/ 6.5km). Just as you leave Burwash, look for the National Trust sign pointing left down a narrow lane leading to **Bateman's** (Saturday to Wednesday, Easter to end October, 11am–5.30pm).

Bateman's was built in 1634 in a lovely situation by the River Dudwell surrounded by rolling hills. Rudyard Kipling lived here from 1902 until his death in 1936 and the rooms in which he wrote many famous works – such as *Puck of Pook's Hill* (1908) and *Rewards and Fairies* (1910) – have been preserved as they were in his lifetime.

After touring the house and gardens, walk down to the watermill, which grinds corn on Saturday, to feel the magic of the spot where Puck appeared to Dan and Una one Midsummer's Eve at the beginning of Kipling's wonderful evocation of English history ('the noise of the mill at work sounded like bare feet running on hard ground. A cuckoo sat on a gatepost singing his broken June tune, "cuckoo-cuk", while a busy kingfisher crossed from the mill stream to the brook . . . the bushes parted . . . they saw a small, brown, broad-shouldered, pointy-eared person with a snub nose...').

Great Dixter, a pleasure for every gardening enthusiast

The National Trust restaurant at Bateman's serves excellent light lunches which you can eat in the garden in fine weather. Alternatively, there are two good pubs on the next stage of our journey. Return to Burwash and retrace your earlier route to Etchingham. The de Etchingham Arms, in the High Street, is a lovely inn beside a trout stream with gardens and good food, including vegetarian dishes. From Etchingham continue to Hurst Green. Turn right on to the A21 and left, after a mile (1.5km), on a narrow lane signposted to Bodiam. Follow this road to its junction with the A229 – 2½ miles/4km. Cross the A229 and carry on for another 2 miles/ 3km, descending via a narrow lane into the village of Bodiam where the Castle pub beside the River Rother serves meals and has a garden for children to play in.

Bodiam Castle (summer 10am–6pm daily; winter 10am–sunset daily except Sunday) is opposite the pub and will delight adults and children alike. Rising romantically from a moat filled with huge carp, it was built in 1385 against an expected French invasion that never occurred. An audio-visual presentation explains its history and the development of medieval armoury. Refreshments can be had in the castle tea rooms before we head off for Great Dixter. From the car park, turn left, cross the medieval bridge over the Rother and follow the winding road for 3 miles (5km) until it climbs up to Staplecross, noting as you go how abundant this lane is with wildflowers. At the Staplecross junction, turn left and follow the B1265 for 3 miles/5km to its junction with the A28. Turn left and continue for 2 miles/3km into **Northiam**; at the centre of this long, straggling village, opposite the village shops and pub, turn left and drive down Dixter Lane to **Great Dixter** (daily except Monday, 1 April to 14 October, 2–6pm last entry 5pm).

Pay your admission at the front porch and check the time of the next tour. While waiting, explore the excellent gardens, with their

Bodiam Castle, twice

imaginative steps and terraces laid out by the great Edwardian architect, Edwin Lutyens, using local red tiles. The gardens have been maintained by Christopher Lloyd since 1954, continuing the work begun by his parents who acquired the house in 1910.

Lloyd is one of England's most innovative gardeners; his books and his weekly magazine articles have inspired many people, as has his pioneering use of wildflowers and so-called 'weeds' in his planting schemes. Throughout the garden you will find unusual plants combined in ways that break with conventional notions but which fire the imagination. The house itself is a beautiful mélange of massive timbers, fine antiques and book-lined walls. Linger in the garden as long as you wish, then head for Rye where we will spend the night.

Return to the centre of Northiam and turn right on to the A28. Follow this road to Broad Oak (4 miles/6.5km) and turn left on the B2089 signposted to Rye. Follow this road to Rye (8 miles/13km) noting the views left over the Tillingham valley and right over the Brede valley to the sea.

Tourist Information/ Accommodation Booking Service
The Heritage Centre,
The Strand, Rye
Tel: 0797-226696
Open daily 9.30am–5.30pm.

Accommodation

BROOMHILL LODGE
Rye Foreign, Rye. Tel: 07978-421
On the A268, 2 miles/3km northwest of Rye, this is a very comfortable country-house hotel with restaurant. Moderate.

FLACKLEY ASH HOTEL
Peasmarsh, Rye. Tel: 079721-651
Country house in quiet grounds on A268, 4 miles/6km northwest of Rye. Restaurant specialising in fish and home-grown vegetables. Swimming pool. Expensive.

GEORGE HOTEL
High Street, Rye. Tel: 0797-222114
Ancient hotel in the heart of Rye with seafood restaurant. Moderate.

HALF HOUSE
Military Road, Rye. Tel: 0797-223404
Pleasant family-run bed and breakfast establishment offering wholefood, vegetarian and vegan food. Free bicycles for the use of guests. Inexpensive.

HOLLOWAY HOUSE
High Street, Rye. Tel: 0797-224748
Set in the heart of Rye and good value. Inexpensive

JEAKE'S HOUSE
Mermaid Street, Rye
Tel: 0797-228828
On Rye's most picturesque cobbled street, quiet, central and furnished with antiques. Moderate.

LITTLE ORCHARD HOUSE
West Street, Rye. Tel: 0797-223831
A beautiful 18th-century house built by Thomas Procter who, as well as being Mayor of Rye, was also a notorious smuggler. Charming decor. Moderate.

THE OLD VICARAGE
66 Church Square, Rye
Tel: 0797-222119
Overlooking Rye's quiet tree-shaded churchyard, right in the heart of the town. Inexpensive.

SALTINGS
Hilders Cliff, Rye. Tel: 0797-223838
A friendly family-run hotel with extensive and delightful views across the River Rother. Moderate.

Concert at Bateman's

Eating Out
Rye has numerous pubs and fish and chip shops serving inexpensive meals based on freshly caught local fish. For more formal dining try any of the following.

THE FLUSHING INN
Market Street, Rye. Tel: 0797-223292
Reservations essential at this very popular restaurant. Outstanding *plateau de fruits de mer* is a speciality of the house. No smoking in the restaurant. Closed Monday, Tuesday, first two weeks of January and June. Expensive.

LANDGATE BISTRO
5–6 Landgate, Rye Tel: 0797-222829
Top quality French cuisine at affordable prices.

If you are prepared to drive 15 minutes or so, there are several pubs in the Rye area where the food is much better than average:

NEW INN
German Street, Winchelsea
Tel: 0797-226252
In Rye's neighbouring Cinque Port town, 2 miles/3km south off the A259, a friendly inn with garden serving fresh fish and homemade pies (accommodation also available).

RAINBOW TROUT
Broad Oak Brede, Tel: 0424-882436
On the B2089, 8 miles/13km west of Rye. Reservations advised. Inexpensive oysters (when in season), lobster, fish and steak.

WHITE HART
Cripps Corner, Staplecross
Tel: 0580-830246
On the B2089, 11 miles/18km west of Rye. Reservations advised Friday and Saturday. Inexpensive steaks, fish and vegetarian meals.

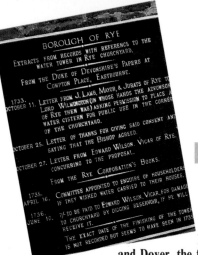

Romney Marsh

Today we will explore the ancient Cinque Port towns of Rye and Winchelsea before driving across the wastes of Romney Marsh to Port Lympne, the Channel Tunnel exhibition and Dover, the final point in our journey.

Rye is one of the jewels of the south coast; an example, rare in England, of a walled hilltop town, it rises out of the flat expanse of Romney Marsh. Rye is one of the ancient Cinque Ports – so called because there were originally five (the number grew to 42 in time) set up to defend England from the threat of invasion from France. In return for maintaining ships of the Royal Fleet in a state of constant readiness, Rye was granted privileges such as freedom from taxation. Despite the defensive walls erected in the mid-14th century, Rye was looted by the French several times. Peace came in the 16th century when the town's harbour began to silt up; Rye is now separated from the sea by a 2 mile/3km expanse of marsh, though small fishing trawlers still come up to the town walls to unload their catch.

Today Rye thrives on tourism and is crowded in summer, though it remains full of charm with its steep cobbled streets lined with picturesque houses. Leave the car in one of the car parks outside the walls and walk up any of the alleys or steps, all of which even-

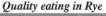
Quality eating in Rye

tually lead to the long High Street. Walk up Lion Street or East Street past the elegant arcaded Town Hall, built in 1743, to the Norman church of **St Mary**, with its splendid clock tower. The two cherubs above the clock face are known as quarter boys because they strike only on the quarter hours. The clock face dates to 1761, but the mechanism is the oldest turret clock still working in England. The church, with its stained glass designed by Edward Burne-Jones in the north aisle, is an atmospheric place to rest while the more energetic climb the tower to enjoy the panoramic views.

The east end of Church Square has a Georgian domed Water House, once used to supply the hilltop town with fresh water. To the left is **Ypres Tower**, built in 1250, and now an excellent museum (Easter to mid-October, 10.30am–1pm and 2.15–5.30pm). The garden below the tower provides views across the marshes to the circular Camber Castle, built by Henry VIII.

Floral decoration

Back in Church Square, leave by West Street and the 18th-century **Lamb House** lies ahead of you. Henry James lived here from 1897 until his death in 1916 and wrote many of his best-known novels in the Garden Room. E F Benson then bought the house and used Rye as the setting for his popular Mapp and Lucia novels. The house is open occasionally (April to end October, Wednesday and Saturday 2–6pm). Continue down West Street and take the first turn left down **Mermaid Street**, Rye's most famous cobbled passage. The **Mermaid Inn**, built around a central courtyard circa AD1500, was the haunt of a notorious gang of smugglers. Stop here for coffee and admire the huge Tudor fireplace and read the information boards charting the town's history. From Mermaid Street descend to Strand Quay where several old riverside warehouses have been turned into shopping arcades selling antiques and local pottery.

You can continue to browse in Rye's many shops and stop for lunch in one of its good pubs, or take the A259 out of Rye for 2 miles/3km to **Winchelsea**. The original town lay on the coastal plain where, battered by the seas, it was destroyed by a great storm in 1280. New Winchelsea was built in 1283 as a port, intended as the main entry point of wines from France, and laid out on an ambitious scale with a street plan of 39 rectangular blocks. Housing plots were let to merchants who built fine houses with capacious wine cellars. The sea receded, Winchelsea was left landlocked and went into genteel decline. A 20-minute stroll will reveal that many of the pretty Georgian houses covered in rambling roses have grilles at pavement level leading to their medieval wine vaults.

Summer retreat, Port Lympne

The **museum** in the 14th-century Court Hall in the High Street illustrates the town's history (May to September, 10.30am–12.30pm and 2.30–5.30pm).The huge church of St Thomas, intended as the centrepiece, was never completed but is still rich architecturally and contains the 14th-century tombs of several knights and admirals of the Cinque Ports. For lunch try the **New Inn** on German Street, an 18th-century pub serving bar snacks or full meals, including freshly caught fish.

From Winchelsea, head back to Rye along the A259, follow the one-way system round the town and turn left on the A268 signposted to Peasmarsh and Northiam. Very soon, just over the railway bridge, turn right down a narrow lane signposted to Appledore. Along this road for the next 7 miles/11km, look out for the remains of eroded cliffs on the left; you are driving along what was – until Saxon times – the seabed. To the right is the vast expanse of **Romney Marsh** – 50,000 acres/20,000ha in extent – created by the silting up of the shallow seabed, leaving a flat region of salt marsh noted for its birdlife, giant frogs and Romney Marsh sheep, prized by gourmets for the salty (*pré-salé*) flavour of the meat. Also on your right is the Royal Military Canal, dug from Rye to Hythe

Romney Marsh, formed by the silting up of the sea

in 1804 to enable troops to move quickly across this difficult terrain as part of England's defences against Napoleon. You are likely to see ducks, geese, swans and seagulls – as well as a solitary heron lazily flapping across the marshes – as you drive towards the pretty village of Appledore. From here, the fastest route to Port Lympne is the B2080 for 4 miles/6km, left in Brenzett on the A2070 for 5 miles/8km, left in Hamstreet on the B2067 and continue for 10 miles/16km until you see the entrance to Port Lympne on the right.

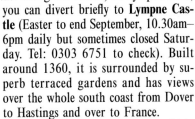

Port Lympne (summer 10am–5pm, winter 10am–dusk) was built for the politician Sir Philip Sassoon between 1911 and 1913 and was one of the last great country houses constructed in England. It was renowned as the social centre of its day and played host to leading figures such as Charlie Chaplin and Sir Winston Churchill. Designed as a luxury summer retreat, the magnificent rooms, including the Tent Room, painted by Rex Whistler, reflect the aesthetic taste of the 1920s. The outstanding terraced garden leads down from the house and the 270 acre/100ha park is now a safari park specialising in endangered species such as elephants, rhinos, tigers and lions.

A mile or so (1.6km) further along the B2067, in Lympne itself,

you can divert briefly to **Lympne Castle** (Easter to end September, 10.30am–6pm daily but sometimes closed Saturday. Tel: 0303 6751 to check). Built around 1360, it is surrounded by superb terraced gardens and has views over the whole south coast from Dover to Hastings and over to France.

In 1993 England and France will be linked again by the Channel Tunnel. If you want to see the **Eurotunnel exhibition**, take the B2068 out of Lympne for 1 mile/1.6km; join the A20 to Folkstone, follow it for 6 miles/10km until you come to the A20/M20 intersection and follow the signs. The exhibition (Tuesday to Sunday, summer 10am–6pm, winter 10am–5pm) shows, by the use of videos and models, how the tunnel is being constructed and how the shuttle system will work.

Alternatively, carry on along the A20 for another 10 miles/16km to **Dover** and our journey's end. You can park in the multi-storey car park in St James

Dover Harbour

Street, behind the Moat House Hotel. Walk up Cannon Street and into Market Square. Here you will find the **White Cliffs Experience** (April to 7 July 10am–6.30pm, 8 July to 1 September 10am–7.30pm, winter opening Tel: 0304 214566). The museum covers Dover's history from Roman times to World War II through a series of animated and noisy tableaux. Among the razzamatazz is a lot of fascinating detail and the excavated remains of Roman buildings.

Tourist Information/ Accommodation Booking Service

Townwall Street, Dover
Tel: 0304-205108
Open summer 9am–10pm, winter 9am–6pm.

Accommodation

BEAUFORT HOUSE
18 East Cliff Marine Parade, Dover
Tel: 0304-216444
Part of a terrace of attractive 19th-century houses set below the castle. Inexpensive.

DOVER MOAT HOUSE HOTEL
Townwall Street, Dover
Tel: 0304-203270

Modern, centrally located hotel. Convenient for exploring the town and resting the night before crossing the Channel. Expensive.

ROYAL HOTEL
Beach Street, Deal. Tel: 0304-375555
18th-century hotel situated right on the beach in Deal, 8 miles/5km north of Dover. The restaurant specialises in fresh fish. Ideal retreat for the last night before going home. Moderate to expensive.

WHITE CLIFFS HOTEL
Waterloo Crescent, Dover
Tel: 0304-203633
Extensive harbour and seafront views. Moderate to expensive.

Eating Out

LE RENDEZVOUS
Cliffe Court Hotel,
East Cliff, Dover
Tel: 0304-211001
Excellent French restaurant with superb balcony views.

WALLETT'S COURT
St Margaret's Cliffe, Dover
Tel: 0304-852424
Gourmet five-course menu at weekends; short set-price menu during the week. Always outstanding. Treat yourself before you go home.

The weathering effect of the sea

Shopping

Fantastic shrimps!

The world is definitely divided into those who love shopping and those who loathe it. If you are one of the former, devote your energies to Tunbridge Wells which is the best shopping town in southeast England. From the Pantiles at the lower end of the town to the Crescent Road/Church Road crossroads at the top of the hill, Tunbridge Wells's half-mile long High Street is lined with small speciality shops: numerous booksellers selling new and secondhand publications, antique shops specialising in dolls, toys, clocks and scientific instruments, shops selling Italian interior design or oriental carvings and silks and every type of clothing from Loden coats (Fox Brothers in the Pantiles) to chic, one-off evening gowns.

Rye is another town that will appeal to browsers and serious buyers, with the best shops at either end of the High Street. At the Landgate end, just within and beyond the town walls, are good antique shops where you will need a fat bank balance to afford the top-quality furniture and oil paintings. Modern art and crafts come cheaper at the Rye Art Gallery (107 High Street). At the other end of the High Street, which leads to the Mint and Strand Quay, every other shop deals in small, portable antiques and locally made ceramics, and more affordable, but less portable, pine and reproduction furniture (some shops will handle shipping for you).

The Martello Bookshop (26 High Street) stocks a comprehensive collection of books about the region or by local authors. It is also the headquarters of the Tilling Society, made up of people who know and love E F Benson's comic Mapp and Lucia novels, three of which are set in Rye, and which are worth reading for an insight into small town politics and petty rivalries.

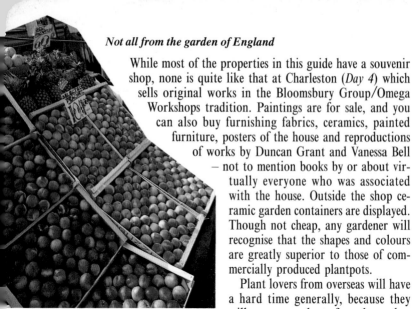

Not all from the garden of England

While most of the properties in this guide have a souvenir shop, none is quite like that at Charleston (*Day 4*) which sells original works in the Bloomsbury Group/Omega Workshops tradition. Paintings are for sale, and you can also buy furnishing fabrics, ceramics, painted furniture, posters of the house and reproductions of works by Duncan Grant and Vanessa Bell – not to mention books by or about virtually everyone who was associated with the house. Outside the shop ceramic garden containers are displayed. Though not cheap, any gardener will recognise that the shapes and colours are greatly superior to those of commercially produced plantpots.

Plant lovers from overseas will have a hard time generally, because they will see many plants for sale as they tour the gardens in this guide that cannot legally be taken home because of Customs and Excise restrictions. My advice is to check whether the nursery or garden provides a mail-order export service. If not, write down the names of the plants you covet and then buy a copy of *The Plant Finder* from any good bookshop. In this bible of the English garden world you are bound to find a nursery listed that will supply export orders.

If you cannot take home plants, you can at least fill your car boot with English wines. Wine grapes were introduced to Britain by the Romans and many a vineyard was planted by the Normans. A prolonged period of cold wet weather in the 13th and 14th centuries put paid to vine cultivation and thereafter vines were regarded as an expensive luxury for hothouse cultivation. Cynics regarded the first attempts at establishing commercial vineyards in England in the early 1950s as harebrained and doomed to failure but hard work paid off when the two hot summers of 1975 and 1976 produced wines that won prizes in Europe in competition with French and German products, and the two summers of 1989 and 1990 saw further good vintages.

English wine-makers have learned a great deal over the last fifteen years and are producing blends influenced by the 'New World' wines of California and Australia. Some of the best and longest established vineyards are located in southeast England and many more

Old and pricey souvenirs

Local wickerwork

are being planted. Competition is driving prices down to a more reasonable level and you may pick up bargain-priced wine direct from the producer if you buy in quantity.

To sample the best of the region's products, call at Lamberhurst Vineyards (*Day 3*), Sheffield Park (*Day 4*) or the English Wine Centre at Alfriston. Alternatively, you could do a mini wine-tasting tour while you are in the Battle area (*Day 5/6*). From Battle, drive up the High Street and take the first turn left, Mount Street. Follow this road for 2 miles/3km until you come to Leeford Vineyard, in the valley of the River Brede (Easter to Christmas Eve, Monday to Saturday 10am–5.30pm, Sunday noon–5.30pm). This 35-acre/14ha vineyard produces four wines: medium dry white and rosé, a drier white and a dry Schonburger-grape white called 'Battle'.

Fruit, veg and videos

Turn right out of the vineyard and take the first right turn which leads to the A21. Cross the main road and continue on to Spilsted Farm to taste and compare the products of this relatively new vineyard. Finally, turn right out of Spilsted, and then left to join the A229. After a mile/1.6km, on the left, is Sedlescombe Organic Vineyard where you will receive a warm welcome from the owners.

Here you can taste and buy Sedlescombe's own organic wines, including a sparkling 'champagne'. If you end up exhausted after touring the vineyards and the woodland nature trail, you can always spend the night (for advance bookings Tel: 0580 830715).

Eating

Pubs & Restaurants

In the *Day Tours* section of this guide I have recommended specific places to eat. About half the recommendations are pubs rather than restaurants, and this is deliberate because pub food represents good value for money. Pubs, with their lower overheads, are cheaper

Oyster feast

than restaurants, and their informality is part of the pleasure; you don't have to dress up, you can have as many, or as few, courses as you wish and you don't have to buy a bottle of overpriced wine. Some pubs do have dining areas set aside with waiter/waitress service, but in most the arrangements are less formal; daily specials are chalked up on a blackboard and you order your food at the bar; in some pubs the food will be brought to your table, while in others you collect it from the bar.

The staple of pub menus at lunchtime is the 'Ploughman's Lunch', an invention of marketing men in the 1960s designed to promote English cheese. If only the cheeses were always English, or better still, local! A ploughman's lunch of fresh-baked bread, local cheese, homemade tomato chutney and salad is delicious, but some pubs still tend to serve an unadventurous choice of 'cheddar', unripe brie and chalky, immature Stilton.

Grilled pork or beef sausages, served with bread and mustard, are more likely to be locally made, good and meaty, since many butchers in the region make their own, and you may come across unusual varieties flavoured with pine nuts, apricots and herbs, or

Necessary refreshment

others made from lamb, wild boar or venison. Lunchtime menus will also feature cold pork or chicken and ham pies and such pub staples as shepherd's pie, macaroni with cheese sauce, and lasagne.

Evening menus are often more adventurous. Fish and seafood will feature on many menus, since the sea is never very far away. You are increasingly likely to be offered oysters at affordable prices. The small, sweet, smooth-shelled oysters – Colchesters and Whitstables – are still rare and expensive delicacies, but Pacific, or Portuguese oysters, larger, with crinkly encrusted shells, are more resilient, and being farmed in growing quantities on the north Kent coast, around Whitstable.

Fish is becoming more expensive, but the flat fish of English inshore waters – sole, dab, plaice – are delicious grilled with butter and herbs, especially when they have been caught within the last 24 hours. Farmed salmon and trout are now so cheap they no longer count as luxury foods, and although the farmed version is not so tasty as the wild, they still make a satisfying and wholesome dish.

Every year surveys into the eating habits of the English reveal that the top choice, when eating out, is grilled steak. It is therefore an unusual pub that does not offer a choice of rump steak, sirloin or T-bone. Many pubs in the region are supplied by local butchers who know how to age and cut their meat for maximum taste and you will soon know, if you order steak, whether you have found one of those or not. Vegetarians no longer need to face the fear of starvation when they eat out. Only about two years ago the standard response to a request for vegetarian food was an omelette with limp lettuce salad. Suddenly all that has changed, at least in this part of England. Most of the region's pubs and restaurants now

have a section of their menu devoted to vegetarian dishes that are often more imaginative than the meat alternatives.

Pubs have been forced to diversify into serving food and non-alcoholic drinks to stay in business. Even so, non-drivers should take the opportunity to sample beers, wines and ciders. Traditional English bitter beer is a nutty, golden brown in colour and quite strong in contrast to Continental beers. The flavour depends on the amount of hops that are added during fermentation – the more hops, the more bitter the beer, but the stronger the fragrance. A local brewer, Harveys of Lewes, supplies many of the pubs in the area and there are few better beers than theirs.

Southeast England is fruit and apple country and Merrydown, based at Horam in East Sussex, is one of the country's biggest cider makers. Their vintage cider is dry, sparkling and almost good enough to pass comparison with champagne. Merrydown also makes English fruit wines from elderflowers and elderberries, plums, damsons and gooseberries – all on the sweet side but ideal as a *digestif* or dessert wine. The region's mild, maritime climate has resulted in a renaissance in wine making and several local vineyards have won top European awards for their products. Many pubs sell these wines by the glass, providing an ideal opportunity to sample the products of several vineyards in one evening. Most of the grape varieties grown here are of German origin – predominantly Müller Thurgau, Huxelrebe and Reichsteiner.

From the sophistication of wine to the most plebeian food of all: fish and chips. You shouldn't leave the region without trying England's most quintessential dish. Nutritionists argue about whether it is good for you, but nothing beats it for a cheap treat.

The best place to try them would be Rye (*Day 7*) where every

Big plate, small appetite

other restaurant serves them, but the authentic version of fish and chips can only be enjoyed in the open air. Go down to the fish and chip shop on the corner of Wish Street and Strand Quay, buy your meal and cross to the waterside, where you can sit with the wind in your hair, seagulls wheeling overhead and fishing boats moored in the small harbour. The freshness of the outdoors and the salt-laden air will add piquancy to a dish that has found universal favour with just about everyone.

74

Nightlife

Concerts & Theatre

Several historic houses and gardens are used as venues for evening entertainment in the summer. You will usually have to book tickets in advance, but it is worth asking at tourist information centres whether tickets are still available on the day.

Leeds Castle has open-air concerts at the end of June and the beginning of July. Most years top jazz bands perform at the Leeds Castle Open Air Jazz Proms at the end of August (tickets for these events can be bought at Leeds Castle or Tel: 0622 880008 for information and credit card bookings).

The National Trust mounts an imaginative programme of summer events at several of its properties. You are advised to book in advance (write to the Box Office, The National Trust, Scotney Castle, Lamberhurst, Kent TN3 8JN or Tel: 0892 891001 for an events calendar and booking form). Highlights include concerts in July in the gardens of Ightham Mote, Shakespeare or opera against

Open-air concert at Leeds Castle

the backdrop of Scotney Castle in late August, and the four-day Knole Festival of music and drama at midsummer (24 June).

English Heritage puts on events such as international longbow competitions and a recreation of the Battle of Hastings plus summer concerts and opera evenings. For a copy of their Events Diary and booking details write to English Heritage, Keysign House, 429 Oxford Street, London W1R 2HD or Tel: 071-973 3000.

Major Venues

In Canterbury or Chichester, check what is on in the cathedrals: during the summer you will often find evening performances of organ, choral and orchestral music. Otherwise the main entertainment centres in the region are as follows:

Canterbury
Canterbury has two good theatres providing a range of entertainment, including modern dance and ballet, pop, folk and classical music, musicals, comedy and classical theatre: the Gulbenkian The-

Fireworks at the Canterbury Festival

atre, University of Kent at Canterbury (Tel: 0227 769075) and the Marlowe Theatre, The Friars (Tel: 0227 767246). Visit the information centre to book. The Canterbury Festival takes place in mid-October (Tel: 0227 452853).

Sevenoaks

The Stag Theatre in London Road (Tel: 0732 450175) puts on a mixed programme of music, drama and film.

Tunbridge Wells

ASSEMBLY HALL THEATRE,
Crescent Road,
Tunbridge Wells.
Tel: 0892 30613.
Leading UK ballet and theatre companies and top orchestras.

TRINITY THEATRE
Church Road
Tunbridge Wells
Tel: 0892 544699
Lunch-time concerts and a varied evening programme of poetry, drama, jazz, folk and classical music.

Lewes/Brighton/Chichester

Brighton (12 miles/20km southwest of Lewes, easily reached by car or train) is the southeast coast's main holiday resort and consequently has a range of entertainments, from sophisticated nightspots to cinemas and theatres. Further afield, Chichester's Festival Theatre is renowned for top-class summer productions. The Tourist Information Office in Lewes will help you make bookings. (Although the famous Glyndebourne Opera is just outside Lewes, you are unlikely to get tickets, which sell mainly to subscribers.)

Arts and music festivals take place in Eastbourne and Brighton in May, Chichester in July and Arundel in August. The Lewes Bonfire Night celebrations (5 November) are among the most spectacular in England and feature a costume parade in the High Street.

Interlude at Ightam Mote

Concerts and Theatre

BRIGHTON DOME
27 New Road
Brighton
Tel: 0273-674357
The major entertainment complex in the city; all kinds of events take place here, ranging from international orchestras to rock concerts and stage drama featuring television stars.

NIGHTINGALES
29 Surrey Street, Brighton
Tel: 0273-29086
Theatre pub staging alternative/fringe productions.

THEATRE ROYAL
New Road, Brighton
Tel: 0273-28488
Elegant Victorian theatre staging touring productions.

SALLIS BENNY THEATRE
Grand Parade, Brighton
Tel: 0273-608020
Experimental theatre and concerts.

Discos/Nightclubs

ASYLUM
11 Dyke Road, Brighton
Tel: 0273-727721
Smart and stylish disco.

CASABLANCA
2–5 Middle Road, Brighton
Tel: 0273-21817
Live jazz; relaxed and casual.

MIDNIGHT BLUES
Grand Hotel, Kings Road,
Brighton
Tel: 0273-596660
Up-market nightclub, popular with local people.

Battle/Hastings
Hastings, the seaside resort 10 miles/16km south of Battle, is one of the south coast's main entertainment centres – the concerts and shows are determinedly middle-of-the-road. Contact the White Rock Theatre, Hastings (Tel: 0424 722753) and the De La Warr Pavilion, Bexhill-on-Sea (Tel: 0424 212022), or ask at the Battle tourist office for help with bookings and for the monthly *Hastings Revue*, which covers the more serious arts in the region. The Battle Festival of arts and drama is held every May.

Dover
There is a full programme of summer events ranging from medieval tournaments at Dover Castle to concerts and plays in the Town Hall. Ring the Events Hotline for details (Tel: 0304 375792).

Calendar of Special Events

January to March

During the coldest, darkest and wettest months of the year it is difficult to induce people out of their homes and the events calendar is not crowded. January is pantomime time when theatres put on shows based on popular fairy tales. They are supposed to be for children but the sexual innuendoes and political jokes keep the adults amused.

Being a Protestant nation, England does not have the great *mardi gras* carnival celebrations of Catholic Europe or southern America. Instead, several villages have pancake races on Shrove Tuesday. Pancakes were traditionally made to use up the last of the season's fat before the fasting season of Lent and participants race with their frying pans, tossing their pancakes in the air.

Easter

The most visible sign of Easter is the vast increase in weekend traffic. Stately homes and gardens open their doors for the first time and visitors flock to those which have especially fine displays of daffodils and spring flowers. At several venues (Leeds Castle and the Whitbread Hop Farm, for example) there are Easter Egg Hunts.

May

Chichester Festival Theatre and Glyndebourne Festival Opera seasons begin. Eastbourne hosts an international folk festival, Brighton holds its International Arts Festival and a rally of veteran commercial vehicles and, at the end of the month, one of

Market in Rye

stalls where you can sample dairy products, wines and ciders. You can buy anything from a shepherd's crook to a combine harvester.

June sees numerous flower festivals based in parish churches. Many private gardens open to the public for a day or two to raise money for local charities and they are well worth visiting. Local newsagents and bookshops sell guides to the gardens.

Car Boot Sales came from America and have really taken off here. Anyone can fill their car boot with unwanted junk, pay a small fee and wait for buyers to come and make an offer. Many artists, craft workers, and antique dealers set up stalls as well.

the areas best agricultural shows take place at Heathfield. The cricket season, which began at the end of April, is now in full swing and you can see village cricket at weekends on virtually any village green, or pay to watch the professional county sides at Canterbury, Hove or Hastings.

June

The season of agricultural shows, the main event being the South of England Agricultural Show and Craft Fair at Ardingly at the beginning of the month. These days rare breeds form part of the show. Leeds Castle has a hot-air Balloon Fiesta early in the month.

The livestock judging is increasingly peripheral to the sideshows and

July

Chichester comes alive with a two week festival at the beginning of the month and there are carnivals in several large towns such as Dover, Maidstone and Ramsgate. Carnival English-style begins with a parade through town. Local clubs and societies compete for prizes for the best costumes and displays and the afternoon ends with a funfair.

August

The homespun village version of carnival is the summer fête. A marquee serving refreshments is set up on the village green or playing field and there are stalls, competitions and contests. It's all good fun and raises lots of money for local charities.

Among more formal events are the Brighton Carnival, the Brighton Great British Beer Festival, and the Arundel Festival of arts. Summer madness builds to a peak with the International Birdman Rally on Bognor Regis Pier where, in defiance of the laws of aerodynamics, partici-

Fairground in Hythe

pants attempt to fly off the pier with elaborate wings and devices strapped to their bodies.

September

With harvest over, this is the season of ploughing matches, which take place at weekends all over the region. There are serious competitions as well as demonstrations of horse-drawn ploughing, veteran farm tractors and steam engines.

Virtually any church you visit this month will be decorated with fruits and flowers for the annual harvest festival, an important occasion in the Anglican church calendar.

October

By mid-October most of the stately homes and gardens admit their last visitors before closing the season. You could spend a day at the races: there are meetings at Folkestone, Brighton, Fontwell and Plumpton during the month.

November

Guy Fawkes night, 5 November, is a big event in several southeastern towns. Guy Fawkes and his Roman-Catholic co-conspirators attempted

to blow up Parliament in 1605. Fawkes was caught and executed. Ever since, on the anniversary of the event, bonfires have been lit and Guy Fawkes's effigy burnt. In Lewes, where anti-Catholic feeling was strong because 17 of the town's leading Protestants were executed under the reign of 'Bloody Mary', the Catholic Queen Mary I, Bonfire Night is still celebrated with fervour. There is a torch-light costume parade through the town with marching bands culminating in a great bonfire, though today the effigy burnt is sometimes of an unpopular political or public figure.

Elsewhere in the region, big public fireworks displays are increasingly popular as an alternative to private parties. If 5 November falls on a weekday, public fireworks displays are held on the nearest Saturday.

November is also the month of the London to Brighton rally, when veteran cars make the 54-mile/86-km journey to raise money for charity.

December

Towns decorate their main streets with coloured lights and Christmas trees, and shops compete with tempting window displays. Local choirs sing carols on the streets to raise money for charity and in Chichester and Canterbury there is fine seasonal music from the cathedral choirs.

The summer game

PRACTICAL Information

via the M23 northbound and the M25

Ferries in Dover Harbour

via the M23 northbound and the M25 eastbound to Junction 5. From Heathrow there is a longer journey along one of the busiest stretches of London's M25 orbital motorway. Take the M4 westbound for 2 miles/3km, then the M25 southbound for 44 miles/70km to Sevenoaks, Junction 5. Alternatively take the Piccadilly line tube into London and catch a train to Canterbury, Sevenoaks, Tunbridge Wells or Lewes where you can pick up a car and begin your journey on quieter roads.

From London City airport, mainly used by business travellers, it is best to head eastwards, along the A13, following the signs for the Dartford Tunnel where you can join the M25 southbound for Sevenoaks (total distance 34 miles/54km). London Stansted airport, extended in 1991 to take longhaul flights, is 50 miles/80km from Sevenoaks; take the M11 southbound and join the M25 southbound to Junction 5.

GETTING THERE

By Air

From any of London's four airports you will only have to drive an hour or two to reach southeast England. Gatwick airport is the closest: only 18 miles/30km to Sevenoaks (*Day 2*)

By Rail

Hourly services link London to several points in the southeast. For information on services and fares call Network Southeast on 071-222 1234 or pick up timetables and route maps

at Travel Centres in any London station. Trains for Canterbury, Sevenoaks, Tunbridge Wells and Battle all depart from Charing Cross. Trains for Lewes depart from Victoria.

By Road

From almost any point in Britain the fastest route to southeast England is by motorway to link up with the M25, which avoids central London. From London itself, however, you can take the A2/M2 to Canterbury.

If you are coming from Portsmouth or Southampton, head for Chichester and take the route detailed in Day 4 Options, along the foot of the South Downs to Lewes, avoiding the heavily congested A27 south coast road.

By Sea

Southeast England is well served by cross-Channel ferries. The fastest crossings are the hovercraft services from Calais to Dover (35 minutes) and Boulogne to Dover (40 minutes) and the Seacat (Calais to Dover 45 minutes, Boulogne to Dover 65 minutes), but these services are liable to cancellation in rough weather. There is a choice of other services:

To Portsmouth from Le Havre (5½ hours), Caen (5¾ hours) and Cherbourg (average 6 hours); around 50 miles/80km to Lewes (*Day 4*) via Chichester.

Dieppe to Newhaven (4 hours); from Newhaven it is 8 miles/13km to Lewes on the A26.

Boulogne to Folkestone (1¾ hours);

16 miles/26km to Canterbury on the A260/A2.

To Dover from Calais (1¼ hours), Boulogne (1¾ hours), Ostend (4 hours), Zeebrugge (4 hours); 16 miles/25km to Canterbury on the A2.

Vlissingen to Sheerness (average 9 hours); 26 miles/42km to Canterbury on the A249/A2.

From Felixstowe and Harwich it is around 110 miles/175km on the A12 via Colchester and Chelmsford to join the M25.

When to Visit

Most houses and gardens are open from Easter until the second week in October, so there will be far less to see if you travel out of season. April, May and September are the least busy times when you are most likely to find hotels without booking. The re-

Evening idyll in East Sussex

gion's gardens are probably at their best in June. July and August are the busiest months and visitors should definitely book in advance.

Visas and Passports

EC visitors enter the UK on a national identity card. Everyone else needs a full passport: visitors from the US, Japan, most Commonwealth and South American countries can enter without a visa.

83

Window in Alfriston Chapel

usually operate on either 240 or 110 Volts. US visitors may need to bring an adaptor for hairdryers, etc.

Time Difference
Greenwich Mean Time is observed from late October to late March, when clocks go forward by an hour for British Summer Time. This means the UK is normally an hour behind Continental Europe, 8 hours behind Singapore and Hong Kong, 9 hours behind Japan, 8 to 10 hours behind Australia and 12 hours behind New Zealand, but 5 hours ahead of the American East Coast and 9 to 11 hours ahead of the West Coast.

Vaccinations
None required.

Customs
The usual duty-free limits, posted at airports and ferry terminals, apply to alcohol, cigarettes and certain toiletries. Visitors' personal possessions are not normally subject to duty but you cannot import narcotics, firearms, plants, animals or raw meat.

Weather
England's maritime climate is very changeable. It is rarely uncomfortably hot, humid or cold, but it can sometimes rain for days on end. Southeast England has a relatively low rainfall, however, and hotter summers than the rest of the UK.

Clothing
Relaxed is the norm, though you will be expected to dress smartly for dinner in restaurants. Rainproof shoes and a light raincoat are a good insurance against unpredictable weather at all times of the year. Warm clothes are essential for winter.

Electricity
240 Volt, 50 cycles AC. Plugs are square, three prong. Shaver points

GETTING ACQUAINTED

Geography
Southeast England is bordered by the Thames estuary to the north and the English Channel to the south. Geologically it is like a sandwich: the North Downs of Kent and the South Downs of Sussex, two parallel ridges of chalk running east-west, form the bread, and the Weald, a heavily wooded area of clay and greens and hills, forms the filling. Both areas are outstanding for wildlife.

Government and Economy
The southeast is politically right of centre, invariably electing Conservative members of parliament although the Liberal Democrats control many of the local councils. The Labour Party has never found a foothold in an area of independent-minded farmers and small businesses. Apart from farming, the economy is geared to the service sector – especially tourism and distribution.

Many residents commute to London to work, and a lot of people in southeast England cross the Channel regularly to shop and take advantage of duty-free concessions. This, plus the large number of Dutch, German and French visitors to the region makes the southeast more European and cosmopolitan than much of Britain, although opinion about the merits or otherwise of the Channel Tunnel is still divided.

Religion

The Church of England still plays a central role in rural life, representing traditional values, even to the non-religious majority. It can also be a social centre as well as playing host to flower festivals, musical recitals and arts festivals. English choral music at its very best can be heard regularly in Canterbury and Chichester cathedrals.

MONEY MATTERS

Currency

The British pound (£) is divided into 100 pence (p). Banknotes of £20, £10 and £5 value are most common and coins come in denominations of £1, 50p, 20p, 10p, 5p, 2p and 1p.

Credit Cards

American Express, Diners Club, Mastercard and Visa are accepted virtually everywhere except in the smallest village stores, although most retailers prefer you to pay cash for low-value purchases. You can also use credit cards to obtain a cash advance at any bank.

Cheques

Travellers' Cheques and Eurocheques denominated in sterling can be used to pay for goods and services, provided that you can produce a passport or some form of identification. Foreign currency cheques can only be cashed at a bank, which will charge a small commission.

Exchange

Banks give the best rates. Use hotels or bureaux de change only in emergency because their rates are poor.

Tipping

About the only people you need to tip are porters (say £1), taxi drivers (10 percent of the fare) and hairdressers (10 percent of the bill). Many restaurants add a 10 per cent service charge and there is no need to leave a further tip. For meals in pubs service charge is not usually included; leave a tip of around 10 per cent if there is waitress service.

Wheatfield in Sussex

GETTING AROUND

The tours in this guide are designed on the assumption that you will travel by car (or by bicycle if you are fit and energetic), since many of the sights are not served by public transport. If you bring your own car from overseas you must have a valid driving licence and adequate third-party insurance. Vehicles drive on the left and you will need to adjust your headlights for night driving. The speed limits are 30mph/48kmh in built up areas, 60mph/96kmh on most other roads and 70mph/112kmh on motorways. Seat belts are compulsory for front seat passengers and driver. If belts are fitted in the rear of

the car they must also be worn.

Drinking and driving is a serious offence which could lead to imprisonment and local police will stop anyone who drives erratically. Otherwise, driving in southeast England is a pleasure; drivers are usually courteous and are used to expecting horses, cyclists, farm vehicles and lost visitors around every bend. Town driving is not such fun and street parking is virtually prohibited between the hours of 8am and 6pm. In public car parks you can expect to pay around 30p–50p an hour.

Car Rental
Avis: 081-848 8733
British Car Rental: 0203 716166
Eurodollar: 0895 33300
Hertz: 081-679 1799
Budget: 0800 181181

Breakdown
On a motorway, look for a white marker sign pointing in the direction of the nearest emergency phone box

which will link you directly to a breakdown service. Otherwise, find a public call box and phone one of the following firms which offer 24-hour assistance:

EuroCars: 0732 355822
Reliance: 0892 39341
Road Runners: 0836 223830

Motorists who belong to clubs or associations affiliated with the AA or RAC should check whether they are entitled to free assistance from these organisations. Don't forget to carry your membership card.

HOURS & HOLIDAYS

Business Hours
Businesses work variable hours between 8am and 6pm, but the main rush hours, when traffic is heaviest, are 8–9am and 4.30–5.30pm.

Shops
Small shops open Monday to Friday 9am–5.30pm and on Saturday mornings and are often closed on either Wednesday or Thursday afternoon. Supermarkets open Monday to Saturday 8am–6pm and until 8pm on Thursday and Friday. Some open on Sunday as well and you will find many smaller shops open on Sunday in tourist areas.

Bank Hours
Standard banking hours are Monday to Friday 9.30am–3.30pm, though some banks open until 4.30pm and many also open Saturday morning from 9.30am–noon.

Public Holidays
Many businesses close for the whole period from 24 December through to 2 January. If Christmas, Boxing Day or New Year's Day fall on a weekend, then the next weekday is taken as a

Thatched roof in Bosham

have a swimming pool and tennis court.

All the establishments listed have been chosen because they are conveniently located for the tours, well-furnished, clean, with good, friendly service. They are also popular and likely to be fully booked if you don't make a reservation.

Tourist Information Centres, listed at the end of each day tour, provide accommodation booking services and staff are generally knowledgeable about the establishments on their books. Tourist centres charge a small fee and usually ask you to pay a deposit of 10 per cent of the room price as confirmation.

public holiday. Otherwise public holidays are as follows:

New Year's Day, 1 January
Good Friday
Easter Monday
First Monday in May
Last Monday in May
Last Monday in August
Christmas Day, 25 December
Boxing Day, 26 December

ACCOMMODATION

Specific recommendations have been given at the end of each day in the *Day Tours* section. These cover a range of price categories:

Inexpensive: less than £30 a night
Moderate: £30–50 a night
Expensive: £50 and above.

Inexpensive usually means bed and breakfast accommodation in a private family house, taking up to six guests a night; some rooms have an en-suite shower and toilet, but you may have to share a bathroom. Breakfast will be provided but not dinner.

Moderately priced establishments are usually guest houses with up to 20 rooms, private bathrooms, a dining room serving breakfast and sometimes dinner, and often a small bar or lounge for guests. Rooms will usually have a TV and telephone.

Hotels usually fall into the expensive category and offer full facilities: many

HEALTH & EMERGENCIES

Tel: 999 in an emergency and ask for police, ambulance, fire or coastguard rescue service, as appropriate.

Chemists/Pharmacies

Chemists are staffed by trained pharmacists who can diagnose minor ailments and recommend appropriate medicines which can be sold over the counter. Some medicines can only be prescribed by a doctor (see *Medical/Dental Services* below). Chemists are found in every town; all display a notice in the window with the ad-

dress and telephone number of that day's late-duty chemist, open after normal shopping hours.

Medical/Dental Services

For urgent treatment go straight to the Accident and Emergency (A&E) department, also called Casualty department, at the nearest hospital. In emergencies telephone 999 for an ambulance. Hospitals are listed in the front section of telephone directories under *Useful Numbers*.

For routine ailments, you can find a doctor or dentist in the yellow Pages Telephone Directory under 'Doctors' and 'Dental Surgeons'. Non-residents will have to pay, so it is worth taking out health insurance – even if you are an EC resident and entitled to a refund of the costs. You can only claim a refund if you have completed the necessary forms in advance.

Crime

In rural southeast England you are unlikely to be a victim of crime but in towns car contents make an easy target for casual thieves. Never leave luggage on a roof rack or valuables visible inside your car and always remember to lock up.

Police

If you are the victim of crime, go to the nearest police station and file a report; you may not be able to make an insurance claim unless you report the theft within 24 hours. Look under 'Police' in telephone directories for locations and telephone numbers.

Toilets

Public toilets, either free or coin-operated, are usually located in town car parks, and major stores also have them for the use of customers.

COMMUNICATION & MEDIA

Post

Postage stamps are sold at many supermarkets and newsagents. The cost of sending a postcard or light airmail letter to EC countries is the same as the UK first-class letter rate. For weightier letters and parcels and mail to the rest of the world go to a post office. Sub-post offices are found in most villages, often doubling as the village store and newsagent. Main post offices, in larger towns, offer a broader range of services, such as Datapost courier services. Normal opening hours are 9am–5.30pm Monday to Friday and 9am–1pm Saturday but sub-post offices may close for one afternoon mid-week.

Telephone

Public phone boxes are found in all towns and most villages, often at or near the post office. They either take coins (10p, 20p and £1) or phone cards which can be purchased in post offices, newsagents and petrol stations. In rural areas, some traditional red call boxes remain, and these are coin operated.

To call a UK number you need to use the area code unless you are dialling within the same area. UK calls are cheapest between 6pm and 8am and at weekends; the standard rate applies from 8–9am and 1–6pm and the peak rate from 9am–1pm.

International calls can be made from all public telephones, which is cheaper than using a hotel phone. International dialling codes and charges are listed in the front of all telephone

Traditional phone boxes

Strictly no parking

and you can tune in to Dutch and French stations on FM.

Admission Charges

Many of the houses and gardens featured in this guide are owned by the National Trust or English Heritage and you can get free entry to their properties by becoming a member. You can join on the spot at any property or write in advance for a membership form to:

THE NATIONAL TRUST
Membership Department,
PO Box 39,
Bromley,
Kent BR1 1NH.
Tel. 081-464 111 for credit card membership by phone.

ENGLISH HERITAGE
Membership Department,
PO Box 1BB,
London W1A 1BB.

At most properties children under five are admitted free; children under 16, students, the unemployed and senior citizens are usually entitled to reduced price admission (and membership) on production of proof of their status.

directories. To call overseas, dial 010 followed by the country code, area code and the number. Dial 100 for the operator if you want to make a collect call/reverse charge call or pay by credit card.

Newspapers and Magazines

In larger towns there will be at least one newsagent stocking major European papers and the European editions of the *International Herald Tribune* and *Wall Street Journal*. If you read English the choice of newspapers and magazines, local and national, is enormous. *The Times*, *The Independent*, *The Guardian* and the *Daily Telegraph* are serious newspapers with a high standard of reporting UK and international news. The *Financial Times* covers world business news and market prices. There are also half a dozen lighter, tabloid national newspapers.

On Sundays, the *Sunday Times*, *Independent on Sunday*, *Observer* and *Sunday Telegraph* bring out hefty editions full of features on travel, property, gardening, the arts and cookery.

Radio and Television

Full programme listings of the four national TV channels and the five national radio stations are carried in daily newspapers and the *Radio Times*. You can listen to pop music on BBC Radio One, light music on Radio Two, serious music on Radio Three, news and talk on Radio Four and sports coverage, plus the BBC World Service, on Radio Five. Local radio stations will keep you in touch with traffic news and events in the region

A racy read

Maps

The routes in this guide are based on major roads, for the sake of simplicity. If you want to get off the beaten track you are advised to buy Ordnance Survey Landranger series maps. Maps 179, 186, 187, 188, 189, 197, 198 and 199 will give you complete coverage of southeast England showing public footpaths, archaeological monuments and topographical features.

Alternatively you can buy the Ordnance Survey Routemaster map number 9, South East England which is less detailed but shows all roads you are likely to need.

Bus-stop in Hastings

FURTHER READING

The *Buildings of England* series is invaluable to anyone interested in architecture. It describes the architectural history and features of every building of merit in the country. There are three volumes covering southeast England.

North East and East Kent, by **John Newman**, Penguin, 1976.

West Kent and the Weald, by **John Newman**, Penguin, 1976.

Sussex, by **Ian Nairn** and **Nikolaus Pevsner**, Penguin, 1973.

If you have children and a stereo system, buy Alan Bennett's highly entertaining tape of *Winnie the Pooh*. The author, **A A Milne**, used Ashdown Forest (*Day 4*) as the inspiration and setting for his stories.

The language of **Rudyard Kipling**'s *Puck of Pook's Hill* is now somewhat archaic, but the story is rivetting and will tell you all you need to know about the history of the region.

H E Bates's Larkin family novels are set in the region. Given wider fame by the TV series *Darling Buds of May*, they are published as an omnibus edition called *The Pop Larkin Chronicles*, by Penguin, 1991.

E F Benson's comic *Mapp and Lucia* novels, several of which are set in Rye, are published by Black Swan and there is an excellent tape recording of the stories read by Prunella Scales.

Virginia Woolf's *Orlando* tells the story of Knole and Vita Sackville-West and is published by Penguin.

Among the best books on the Bloomsbury Group are:

Vanessa Bell, by **Frances Spalding**, Macmillan, 1984.

Charleston Past and Present, Hogarth Press, 1987.

Virginia Woolf, by **Quentin Bell**, 2 volumes, Triad Paperbacks, 1972.

Vita: the Life of V Sackville-West, by **Victoria Glendinning**, Weidenfeld & Nicolson, 1983.

Portrait of a Marriage (Vita Sackville-West and Harold Nicolson), by **Nigel Nicolson**, Weidenfeld & Nicolson, 1973.

Gardens of a Golden Afternoon, by **Jane Brown**, Allen Lane, 1982. One of the best books on Edwin Lutyens and Gertrude Jekyll, whose influence on the region's architecture and gardens was enormous.

For gardens generally, the *Blue Guide: Gardens of England*, A&C Black, 1991, is outstanding.

Art & Photo Credits

Photography **Robert Mort**
Publisher **Hans Höfer**
Design Concept **V Barl**
Designer **Gareth Walters**
Managing Editor **Andrew Eames**
Cartography **Berndtson & Berndtson**

Southeast England

16 km / 10 miles